BASIC BOOKS IN EDUCATIO

Editor: *Kathleen O'Connor, B.Sc., Senior*
Lecturer in Education, Rolle College, Exmouth
Advisory Editor: *D. J. O'Connor, M.A., Ph.I*
Professor of Philosophy, University of Exeter

The Moral Development of Children

This book provides an introduction to the psychology of moral development. The subject is a complex one but a notable feature of the authors' text is the clarity with which they explain the variety of approaches used by different psychologists. These views are summarised in a form which can be readily understood by a student who has little previous knowledge of the technical vocabulary; the authors show that they are complementary rather than conflicting.

The book includes full references to ongoing researches and concludes with a description of the child's overall moral development.

There are summaries and 'further reading' lists at the end of each chapter, a bibliography and an index.

The Moral Development of Children

NORMAN WILLIAMS

RESEARCH FELLOW IN PSYCHOLOGY, FARMINGTON TRUST, OXFORD

and

SHEILA WILLIAMS

RESEARCH ASSISTANT, FARMINGTON TRUST, OXFORD

MACMILLAN

First published 1970 by
MACMILLAN AND CO LTD
London and Basingstoke
Associated companies in New York Toronto
Dublin Melbourne Johannesburg and Madras

Printed in Great Britain by
ROBERT MACLEHOSE AND CO LTD
The University Press, Glasgow

Contents

1 Introduction

Moral development is a complex subject, but it cannot on that account be avoided by those who are going to work with children. The complexity of the subject is due to a number of factors. The words 'moral development' are themselves defined by different people in various ways; and moral behaviour and development are determined by the interaction of a great number of influences, not all of which have been fully described, or investigated, at the present time.

Not everyone is willing to accept the idea that a subject like morality can be approached via evidence and experiment, and some are perhaps still unfamiliar with the idea of psychological evidence itself, not knowing how much weight it carries, or what, in a given instance, is its exact implication. Some, on the other hand, would like naïvely to endow the subject with a quality of authority ('Psychology has proved that such and such').

In fact, most psychologists tended to avoid the subject for many years, and in some areas of the subject, therefore, the evidence is in conflict. In others, there is little evidence, merely an awareness of the nature of the problem. Fortunately, there are areas, too, where the evidence is unambiguous.

This, then, must be a simple book on a difficult topic, a book which does not presuppose a great deal of technical information on the part of the reader. Every effort has been made to avoid clothing the subject with a spurious authority. Where possible, the kind of evidence which justifies particular conclusions has been described. Where the evidence is in conflict, this has been stated. Every effort has been made, too, to ensure that, in simplifying the terminology, and in explaining the background to current work, the issues themselves are not oversimplified.

The limits imposed by the size and the intention of the book rule out an exhaustive review of all the relevant experiments and surveys. Some selection had to be made. This selection was governed in part by a desire to illustrate, for the reader who is new to this field, just how one goes about gathering evidence in this sort of area. The selection reflects, too, the interests of the authors: the book is chiefly concerned with the foundations of moral conduct, and its development in younger children. The moral development of the adolescent is in itself a large enough topic to warrant separate and subsequent study. The sophisticated reader may not agree with the selection. His disagreement may be justified, but the book is not really meant for him: he will have access to the original sources. It is hoped that the reader who is new to the subject will follow up at least some of the titles suggested in the bibliography, so that he may have access to the original sources, too, rather than remain dependent on an introductory volume, such as this.

OBJECTIVE AND SUBJECTIVE JUDGEMENT

Let us look in a little more detail at one of the points mentioned in the preceding section.

It is a sign of one of the changes of interest, which take place from time to time in any subject, that books are being written which, like this one, deal with morality from a psychological point of view. Ten years ago, such books would have been likely to have a rather different emphasis. This would have been apparent in their titles: they would have dealt with topics like social development, adjustment and so on. There was fairly wide agreement that morality was not a proper topic for psychologists. Students of morality – particularly, perhaps, those looking at the subject from a theological point of view – would have said that the subject itself was not amenable to psychological investigation. Psychologists, on the other hand (with a few important exceptions, which we shall discuss later), tended to feel that to take up a topic like morality would in some way compromise their attempts at scientific objectivity. Moral values, it was felt, related to individuals, or to their religions or cultures; to make a moral judgement was, it was said, to make a subjective value judgement. Such a judgement would be almost inevitably ethnocentric, and would therefore lack the proper degree of objectivity.

Although we still respect the need for objectivity, we now tend to think that this position was overstated, and that it contained a number of confusions. In the first place, there is surely a difference between *making* value judgements in the course of your work and taking them as a topic for objective study. In the second place, making value judgements is too insidious a failing to be excluded merely by avoiding certain topics.

Consider, for example, titles like those mentioned above: adjustment, or mental health. Are they really more objective than 'moral development'? It is true that people who write on such topics usually take great trouble to avoid consciously identifying with conventional or religious judgements, but if you look carefully at what they write, you will find that, in many cases, they are making fairly large assumptions as to what an adjusted or a mentally healthy person ought to be like. Such assumptions may reflect the norms of Western societies in which the writers usually grew up, or they may reflect theoretical considerations about the way in which personality functions. In either case, they are likely to be making implicit value judgements. The point is not that this invalidates what is said insofar as it relates to mentally healthy people in our own type of society; it is simply that, although value judgements had the front door slammed firmly in their face, they managed to creep in through the back.

Objectivity, then, is more than a good resolution. It can perhaps best be assured by continual reference to the evidence available, though even in this case, there is room for subjective influences in the *interpretation* of the evidence.

DEFINITIONS

Before going any further; it will be as well to examine the word 'moral' to see what it means and to decide how it will be used in this book. Two main uses of the word may be distinguished. The first of these, which we may describe as the *evaluative* sense, is that which the word has in such phrases as 'He is a moral man', or 'That was a moral thing to do'. It is a usage which carries the implication of the speaker's approval: an action is being judged as good or bad, right or wrong. This usage of the word may be described as one end of a dimension which stretches between moral and immoral. Frequently, in using the word in this way, we are making the sort of subjective value judgements we have already discussed, but this need not always be so. We may restrict ourselves to *describing the characteristics* of that behaviour which can be evaluated as moral, according to the most common usages of the word, and come up with statements of general characteristics which go some way towards being culture-free.

The second meaning of the word may be called the *descriptive* use. This is when we say such things as 'He was faced with a moral choice', or 'This is a moral problem'. In this case, the word is not the opposite of immoral; it simply means 'to do with right and wrong'. The distinction is made clear when we say that a problem of whether to steal or not to steal is a moral one, and whether to walk down to the corner shop or go by bicycle is not. Of course, we are to some extent making a hidden value judgement in assigning some kinds of problem to the category moral and others not, but the broad distinction is probably enough for our present purposes.

It might be convenient if there were actually two words for these usages. Unfortunately, there are not. A little attention to the context, however, will usually show which use any writer or speaker has in mind. Phrases like 'becoming moral' or 'growing into a moral person', 'moral standards' indicate evaluation. Phrases like 'moral judgement', 'moral thinking' are usually descriptive, since they mean 'making judgements which concern the subject of right and wrong', which need not necessarily imply making the right judgements; or, similarly, 'thinking about right and wrong' rather than 'being a right-thinking person'. This applies particularly when the terms are met in psychological literature. It is of course quite possible to use these phrases evaluatively, as you will see if you try changing the emphasis slightly when you say them, but such uses are less common in the work to be discussed here. Phrases like 'moral behaviour' may be used in either way, and careful attention should be given to the context wherever they appear.

It is not suggested that the word should be restricted to only one of these usages. To do so would be quite arbitrary, and it would lead us into difficulties, for however much confusion may be caused by people using the word 'moral' in senses which confuse its two main meanings, the fact remains that the two meanings are there, and they both refer to things we need to talk about. Both senses will then appear at different points in this book. It will usually be clear from the context which one is meant; if not, the meaning will be stipulated.

There is, however, one distinction which will be maintained consistently. This concerns the two terms 'moral education' and 'moral development'. In the first phrase, 'moral' will always be used evaluatively, so we shall understand the term to refer to processes which are set in hand with the aim of making the child moral as opposed to immoral. 'Moral development', on the other hand, will be descriptive. Unfortunately, some people seem to use the term to mean 'causing children to develop in such a way that they believe in what I hold to be right'. In this book, however, it will simply refer to the way in which a child's approach to right and wrong varies as he gets older, whether or not the final stage is usually moral in the evaluative sense. Of course, one hopes that a person does in fact become more (evaluatively) moral as he grows up, but this cannot be taken for granted: we must first look at the evidence.

One general point concerning these two definitions. It is not possible to select either of them as being the proper field of enquiry. Clearly, we cannot study how a child becomes moral without looking at the totality of his approaches to right and wrong. We cannot relate a descriptive developmental study to any practical measures of moral education without knowing which aims we would evaluate as moral ones.

2 Moral Dimensions

We began by asking a number of questions about what we mean by the word 'moral'. Though a necessary beginning, an exercise of this kind is more the concern of the philosopher than of the psychologist. For the latter, this sort of activity is a necessary piece of ground clearing; a precaution, if you like, to make sure that we are in fact investigating the thing that we set out to investigate, and not something else which, owing to a confusion in the way we use words, seems to resemble it. There are similar psychological questions to be asked at the beginning, too. These concern our picture of the actual attributes of the moral person. What kind of attributes are we looking for? How are they likely to be distributed? Are we dealing with simple traits, or complex ones, or with abilities?

But before we can deal with questions like these, we need to clear our minds of a number of popular misconceptions. In the first place, we all have a tendency to ignore the fact that human beings are infinitely variable. It is much simpler to talk as though they can be placed neatly into separate pigeon-holes.

In discussing morality, many of us tend to talk about a 'good man' or a 'bad man', a 'moral person' or an 'immoral' one, as though there were some kind of borderline between these categories. We should not need any knowledge of psychology in the formal sense to reject such a view. And yet such modes of thinking linger, even among those who ought to know better. It was in the last century that the phrase 'a moral imbecile' was coined, but we still hear it from time to time, or equivalent phrases which carry the same image of a discrete group of people, marked off clearly from the rest of the population.

This oversimplified view of human nature tends to linger particularly in the field we are dealing with. It is difficult to see why one should expect people to fall into a few simple categories of goodness and badness. It is certainly not a situation which we find when looking at other human attributes. We cannot sort people simply into the tall and the short. This, of course, is a physical attribute and the error is obvious. But the same situation is to be found with non-physical variables.

Intelligence is a case in point. We may be tempted to classify people as clever, average and stupid, and for many purposes this can provide a rough guide which we can use in our day-to-day life. But consider what happens if we try to apply it too literally. It leads to the assumption that we can have three types of school, one for each category, and that we can allocate people between them by discovering which category they belong to. This sort of arrangement has been tried, as we know, and one of its difficulties has always been that there have been borderline cases who do not fit comfortably into either of two neighbouring categories. Subnormality, too, was once regarded as being a special case. The subnormal were thought to be a sharply demarcated group of people. The study of intelligence, however, has shown that what we are really dealing with is a continuum of intellectual ability, ranging from the genius at one end to the moron at the other. And, as we shall see later, even this view is oversimplifying the problem.

This kind of model of human characteristics is by no means confined to characteristics like intelligence, but applies equally to temperament or personality. Extraversion and introversion are terms which give us an example of this. They were conceived of at first as part of a personality *typology*. That is, they were regarded as quite separate categories into which people could be sorted. More recently, however, it has been possible to measure these attributes, and we now see that they are better regarded as *tendencies*, or opposite ends of a continuum. Just as in the case of intelligence or height, if we could examine a large enough population, we would find that every possible position on the extraversion/introversion continuum would be filled.

Many similar examples could be quoted, but these are perhaps enough to make the point. If we describe human behaviour in terms of separate categories of moral and immoral, it would be to suggest that moral character and moral development are, for some reason, quite differently distributed from any other mental or physical attribute which has been examined.

GENERALITY AND SPECIFICITY

There is, however, more to it than this. Even if we abandon the idea of discrete categories and substitute that of a single continuous scale, we may be doing violence to the facts, not only as described in the reports of psychological research, but also as we observe them in our everyday life. Is it true, or even useful, to say that moral character is a single scale, no matter how finely we may subdivide it?

Again, another area of human activity may provide a useful analogy. Intelligence, we have said, is continuously distributed throughout the population, and this is borne out whenever we give an intelligence test to a large population. This is not the place to attempt an accurate definition of the deceptively difficult concept of intelligence; for our present purposes it is sufficient to say that it is associated with certain kinds of problem-solving ability.

An intelligence test is, of course, simply a series of problems which have been devised in such a way that they meet certain rather rigid criteria. Now, if we give a group of people a number of tests, consisting of problems of different kinds – one consists of verbal problems, another of numerical ones, another of mechanical problems, and so on – we find that the test population is not arranged in precisely the same order of ability in each test.

This, of course, is what we would expect from our general observation and from commonsense. In school, a boy may be good at history and bad at chemistry, bad at English and good at maths. This is a case where our everyday experience and our everyday use of language are at variance with each other. We talk about clever people and stupid people as though cleverness were a single over-riding ability. But if this were really so, it would carry over from one type of problem, or kind of intellectual activity, to another. Although there is a limited tendency for this to happen, the concept does not fit the facts very accurately.

A great deal of work has been done on the psychology of intelligence, and it has become quite clear that there are a number of factors involved. As well as the rather abstract general intellectual factor, we have a number of specific abilities – verbal, numerical, spatial and so on. Although a single measure of intelligence can give us a better guide to a person's performance than a crude dichotomous measure (like clever/stupid), if we want to be really accurate we should use a number of scales, which deal with different aspects of ability.

Now, let us apply this to the idea of morality. It applies in two ways.

Firstly, there is the problem which is described in the literature as situational specificity. Is moral behaviour general or specific? Can we regard it as a single over-riding 'ability', or do people vary in the same way as children do when studying different subjects at school? This is a question of fundamental importance, since it affects our whole orientation to the question of moral education and moral development.

Certainly generality is not something which we always see in our day-to-day life. Just as people perform differently when faced with different kinds of intellectual problems, so there is a certain amount of variation in their behaviour when faced with different kinds of moral problems. A man may go in for all kinds of ethically doubtful practices in his business, and yet be scrupulous in his behaviour in other directions. Because someone will get away with whatever he can on his income tax return, we cannot predict that he will have the same attitude towards paying his household bills. Of course, we know people who are scrupulous in both areas, or in neither area, but there are also many people who would do one and not the other. The man who is very considerate of the feelings of his family and friends, who contributes regularly to, say, Oxfam, may also be an inconsiderate tyrant at work.

Examination of the more extreme cases of moral failure which we may find in the record of criminal courts leads to a similar conclusion. Criminals are rarely all-round degenerates. It has often been reported that, if a man is sent to prison for sexual offences against children, he is given a very hard time by his fellow prisoners, most of whom have been convicted for offences against property. They regard the sexual offender's crime with considerable moral indignation, and they certainly would not be likely to do this sort of thing themselves. On the other hand, nor would the sexual offender be likely to go in for robbery with violence, or floating fraudulent companies.

Observations of this kind may be revealing and suggestive, but there have been occasions when they have been misleading. It is therefore always a good thing to subject them to methodical investigation. The best known investigation of this topic was carried out about forty years ago by an American psychological research team, led by Hartshorne and May (3).* They carried out an extremely thorough enquiry into our topic, and used a very large sample of children. Nothing comparable in scope has been done since, and their work, though not recent, is still one of the most important sets of findings that we have available.

Hartshorne and May used a specially constructed battery of tests and ratings, which were designed to assess different aspects of character. Some were concerned with deceit and cheating, and, of course, with their opposite, honesty. Some were concerned with stealing, and others with such traits as co-operation and self-control. The tests were, for the most part, ingeniously constructed; in particular, they were so made that the subjects were able to accept them as part of their everyday experience, rather than as a special test. As we know, in the latter case, people often try to give as good an impression as possible, so that the results are not always accurate.

A few examples will give you an idea of the way in which Hartshorne and May went about this work. A child was sent to buy something and, by pre-arrangement, he was given too much change. A record was kept of how he responded to this. In another experiment, children were given what appeared to be an ordinary class test. They were later allowed to mark this themselves, not knowing that a record had been made of their original answers, so that cheating by altering answers could be detected.

The rationale of the investigation was simple: if, say, honesty were a general trait, then we would expect the tests described

* Numbers in parentheses refer to Bibliography, pages 115 ff.

above, and the many others like them, to have high positive correlations with each other. That is to say, there would be a tendency for those children who scored highly on one test to score highly on the others: or to put it another way, that there would be a high degree of predictability between one test result and another.

The account of this work, when published, ran to three large volumes, and so it is not possible to give here more than the barest sketch either of the procedures or the findings. Unfortunately, it will be difficult for the reader to get a more detailed picture; the work is now out of print, and it is a fairly uncommon possession even in specialist libraries. A new edition, or an abridgement, has long been overdue. Two conclusions, however, relate closely to what we are discussing here.

1. The distribution of the children's test scores on all the scales confirmed what we have thought to be the likely distribution of moral traits, namely that they do not fall into discrete categories, but can be represented on a continuum, in which every position may be occupied.
2. Concerning the question of general or specific moral traits, the intercorrelations between the tests, though positive, tended to be low. This meant that it was not possible to use a child's response in one moral situation to make an accurate prediction of his performance in another. The authors concluded therefore that moral behaviour is characterised by its specificity.

Since then, a number of people have disagreed with this interpretation, while accepting the procedures on which it is based. Factor analytic studies, using more sophisticated statistical techniques than were available to the original authors, have suggested the existence of a weak general factor of morality, which is common to all the tests. More recently, Eysenck has put forward a more extreme argument (4). Complete specificity, he argues, would lead to intercorrelations around zero; the fact that the correlations were all positive is sufficient for us to reject the hypothesis of specificity. This is perhaps overstating the case.

Now, many readers of this book are likely to be unfamiliar with the interpretation of statistics of this sort. It is probably worth while, then, to explain in non-statistical terms just what is

B

implied, especially as this sort of evidence is quite common in this subject, and in fact this same point about the meaning of low correlation coefficients will come up again in another chapter. The reasoning behind the interpretation of such figures is simple and straightforward. Correlation measures the extent to which two things are associated, or to put it another way, the degree to which you can predict one thing from knowing another. If beauty and brains were highly correlated (nearly 1·0), we could predict the results of a beauty contest by looking at the candidates' IQs. This high degree of association could go either way. It could be that those with the highest IQs were the most beautiful, in which case we have positive correlation, or the most beautiful could be the least intelligent, in which case the correlation is negative. But in either case, the use of either a beauty or an intelligence scale would enable us to predict how a number of girls would rate on the other one, and the prediction would have a fair degree of accuracy. But if (as is probably really the case) the correlations are around zero, indicating no connection between the two attributes, we cannot make accurate predictions of this sort. However – and this is an extremely important point which is often misunderstood – this does not mean that our answers are all wrong; such a state of affairs would show that there was a very high degree of association, but that we have been making the wrong predictions – using our scale the wrong way round. If there is no correlation, we would expect our predictions to be right about as often as would happen by chance – in our example, about fifty per cent of the time.

Let us apply this to the question of generality and specificity. If moral behaviour were completely general, we would be able to predict with accuracy from any one moral situation to another. If a person is moral or immoral in running his business, knowledge of this would enable us to say whether he would be moral or immoral in running his home. But we have seen that the correlations reported, though positive, were low. We now know what this means. If you were to try making a large number of predictions of this sort, you would be right in *more than half* of your judgements – say about 60 to 70 per cent of the time.

We can see, then, what Eysenck meant. This kind of figure

means that for a very considerable proportion of the time an individual may be expected to behave in accordance with his general moral character. But we must not forget about the times represented by the remaining 30 to 40 per cent. Though these are in a minority, they are a substantial minority, indicating that there are nevertheless many occasions on which the person's actions are *not* in agreement with his general moral character.

The trouble is that people tend to try and solve questions of this kind by treating them as though they presented us with simple alternatives, as though they were topics for a debating society where you have to vote for or against the motion. In fact, moral behaviour is characterised both by generality and specificity.

How is this possible? It is by no means contradictory if we suppose the existence of a general factor which is not the only determinant of moral behaviour. We may find, for instance, that morality resembles intelligence, in that there is a general factor which operates in combination with a number of specific ones. The difference in this case seems to be, on any interpretation of the Hartshorne and May results, that the general factor of morality is very much less influential as compared with its specific factors than is the case with the general factor of intelligence.

This degree of specificity may be accounted for in two ways. Firstly, the individual's response may be governed by particular environmental situations. He does not count, for instance, some things as being a matter of moral behaviour, and therefore does not apply the rules to them. This is possibly the case where we find otherwise honest people fiddling their tax returns, or getting extra bottles of brandy or extra cartons of cigarettes through the customs. Or we may find that people have different sets of rules which they apply to different situations. A child may have one morality in school, another at home and yet a third when playing with the gang.

Secondly, it may be that morality is not a simple personality trait. The comparison between the specificity findings and the structure of intelligence may help us here. If moral behaviour is determined by some general trait acting in conjunction with a number of specific ones, we may expect that different situations, either in real life or in laboratory tests, might tap different traits, either singly or in combination with each other, in which case the various traits would have different weightings. As we have seen, this is consistent with the evidence, but we need to have more information, and information of a different kind, before the 'traits' or 'factors' become something more descriptive than statistical entities.

COMPONENTS OF MORAL BEHAVIOUR

This brings us to the second main point to be made in this chapter. In the past, there has been a tendency to discuss morality as though it were a single personal attribute which manifested itself in action. This kind of approach has often been associated with attempts at moral education. It has been assumed that morality consists of having the right beliefs, or the right values, and moral education has been regarded as being essentially concerned with the inculcation of such values, or even the indoctrination of the right beliefs.

But this must surely be an extremely naïve view. It is not by any means true that, if a person believes the right thing, he will also behave in the right way. A man may believe quite sincerely that it is wrong to punch someone on the nose, and yet he may physically attack people every time they offend him. He may be said to be lacking in some quality, such as self-control, which is necessary for putting his principle into practice. Again, a person may believe that he should comfort the distressed, that it is a pressing moral duty to do so. He may, however, consistently fail to carry this out. He is, perhaps, unable to recognise which people are distressed, or he may be so socially inept that those people he tries to comfort become far more distressed than they were in the first place. We would perhaps hesitate to describe such a person as immoral, but it is clear that he is, at the least, morally ineffective.

Moral behaviour, then, is a more complex matter than simply subscribing to a set of values. The individual needs certain attributes in order to put his morality into effect. Morality is not something simply to be believed, but also something to be put into practice. To call a person 'moral' it is not enough to say that he has good intentions; on the other hand, it is not sufficient to say that a moral person is one who behaves in a particular way; the good intentions are necessary as well.

We have seen from the foregoing examples that moral behaviour may involve a number of different components. In these two examples alone we can distinguish: a factor of belief or principle; some degree of empathy or insight into other people's feelings; an ability to predict the consequences of one's actions: a quality of self-control; and social or interpersonal skills.

John Wilson, Director of the Farmington Trust Research Unit into Moral Education, has constructed a conceptual model of the attributes of the morally-educated person, which describes a number of components (5).

One difficulty which faces the author of a scheme such as this is that apparently appropriate words like 'concern' or 'rationality' are already so loaded with meanings carrying over from other people's use of them that they may become a barrier to, instead of a means of, communication. All too often the reader has such fixed ideas about what such words mean that he does not wait to discover what it is that the author is trying to say.

Wilson got round this problem by making up new names for his components: easily remembered monosyllables which derive from Greek roots, the meanings of which are connected with the characteristics of the various components. The components are: PHIL, EMP, GIG, DIK and KRAT.

PHIL refers to an *attitude* in virtue of which other people's feelings, wants and interests actually count or weigh with one, or are accepted as of equal validity to one's own. It seems likely that two variables may be distinguished. Individuals may differ with regard to the number of persons or groups to whom the subject's ascription of equality applies; we are referring to this as the *range* of PHIL. Individuals may also be differentiated on a dimension which is something like 'strength of conviction'; we are referring to this as *strength* of PHIL.

In these discussions of PHIL, 'equal' means simply that the subject regards others as having the same rights as himself, and entitled to equal consideration. It is not *logically* necessary that the subject should feel any particular affection for the other (though it may be the case that such feeling is, or has been, necessary for the development of this attitude).

PHIL may best be regarded as an attitude or orientation towards other people, rather than as necessarily implying the existence of a consciously formulated principle in all cases.

EMP refers to an *ability*, namely awareness or insight into one's own and other people's feelings: that is, the ability to know what those feelings are and describe them correctly.

GIG refers to an attainment, viz. the mastery of relevant factual knowledge. To make correct moral decisions, PHIL and EMP are not sufficient: one also needs to have a reasonable idea of what consequences one's actions will have, and this is not entirely a matter of EMP. Thus a person might have enough EMP to know that a Negro's experience of pain is like that of a white person, and enough PHIL for this to count with him in making moral choices: but, through sheer ignorance rather than lack of EMP, he might believe that (say) Negroes have less nerve-endings or thicker skulls and therefore they do not get hurt so easily. Similarly, Marie-Antoinette ('let them eat cake') may have lacked GIG rather than EMP or PHIL.

Social skills also refers to an attainment, but one which is a matter of 'knowing how' rather than 'knowing that' (the latter is GIG). We are here concerned primarily with competence at playing the social and interpersonal roles that a person may choose to have imposed on him. Thus among people with the same amounts of EMP, PHIL, etc. some will be more successful than others at letting the other person see that they care, sympathise, understand, etc., and at doing something effective to help him.

DIK refers to the rational formulation of EMP and GIG, on the basis of PHIL, into a set of rules or moral principles to which the individual commits himself, by the use of such universalising words as 'good', 'right', etc. where these rules relate to other people's interests. There may be people good at PHIL, EMP and GIG, who nevertheless do not put all these together to make a set of consistent and action-guiding principles, or who draw their moral (or pseudo-moral) principles irrationally from elsewhere.

KRAT covers those factors or attributes which enable a person to bring his other moral attributes (PHIL, EMP, GIG, etc.) to bear on a situation: those which, firstly, *alert* him to the situation and motivate him to think about it in a morally educated way, and secondly those attributes which enable him subsequently to translate his decision into appropriate action. These attributes might roughly be described as those which make for *resolution*.

If these components are to help us in examining the psychology of moral development, we must be quite sure that we understand exactly what they represent. It would be tempting to regard each one as being a unitary psychological trait, but a moment's thought will show that this is not necessarily so. A conceptual model such as this lists the qualities that are necessary – the things a person has to be able to do – in order to count as moral. But we are not entitled to translate these requirements on a simple one-to-one basis into psychological characteristics.

Perhaps a simpler example than morality will make this clear. We may say that the logical requirements for a *punctual* person include: being able to tell the time; being able to organise his journeys; a respect for other people's feelings, since otherwise he would not mind keeping them waiting; and of course he must also have a watch or a clock, or at least be able to see one when necessary. When we come to translate these into psychological terms, we find we have rather a mixed bag. Telling the time is a fairly simple skill, which can be treated as a unitary trait for purposes of testing it, but developmentally it is itself loaded with other skills such as reading, knowing the numbers and having certain concepts to do with space and motion. These latter concepts must also play a part in the individual's ability to get himself to the right place at the right time. Respect for other people, on the other hand, may well prove to be a unitary character trait. As for the last requirement, it is not in any sense a psychological attribute at all, though it may indirectly be connected with a sociological one.

The same holds good for the components of morality. EMP is fairly clearly a skill of some kind, though rather a complex one in psychological terms. PHIL is an attitude. The psychological status of the others is more difficult to determine.

But though there may be no one-to-one correspondence, a

model of this sort does serve a very useful purpose in showing us the *sort* of things we are looking for.

A MULTI-DIMENSIONAL MODEL

We are dealing, then, with, in addition to a hypothetical general factor, which we cannot at the moment identify, a number of assorted factors which include cognitive abilities, social abilities and attitudes.

Moral behaviour is thus likely to prove to be multi-dimensional, and any account which is limited to, say, the child's moral thinking, or his moral behaviour, is taking into account one aspect of the subject only.

This is likely to be important both for our view of the structure of moral character – the static view – and for the child's moral development.

To discuss the first of these: you will remember that at the beginning of this chapter we examined the view that morality is distributed along a continuum. If this were all there is to it, it would be easy to assess moral development or the results of moral education, since – at least in principle – individuals could be placed in a rank order, or on a scale of morality, ranging from the most moral to the least. Unfortunately, this is not likely to work in practice.

The components we have discussed are very different in kind. Although it may be that some of them turn out to go together, we must be prepared to find that, in the case of others, there is no necessary connection between the individual's score on one and his score on another; that the intercorrelations of the scores are, in other words, near zero. This, as we have seen, does not preclude the possibility of all-round high scorers; it simply means that accurate prediction cannot be made. The factors are, we would say, orthogonal, or at right angles to each other.

This situation is a familiar one in the psychology of personality. It has been demonstrated clearly in the work on extraversion and neuroticism by Eysenck (4). (See also Cattell (1).) In dealing with a single personality trait, such as extraversion, ranking individuals is a simple enough task: the individual's position appears as a point along a straight line, and it has an unambiguous relationship with all other points as far as a rank order is concerned. But if we introduce a second measure, such as neuroticism, which is orthogonal to the first, we must show the individual's position on two variables at once.

This can only be done by representing him at a point not on a line, but *in an area*, which is defined by the two linear scales placed at right angles to each other. In this case, the idea of putting people into a rank order becomes less helpful. True, those cases where the same kind of score is recorded for both variables may be placed fairly clearly with regard to each other and the rest of the population. But the other cases, where a higher score is obtained on one variable than on the other, cannot be ranked unless we make a value judgement and say that one of the variables is more important. What we cannot do is add them together and treat them as a single score.

Suppose now that we add a third variable, and that this is orthogonal to the other two. In this case, the positions of individuals relative to each other can be represented as points in three-dimensional space – a cube defined by the three measures we are concerned with. Here again, high scorers and low scorers on all three measures are differentiated fairly clearly, but the position remains ambiguous for those with intermediate, mixed results.

This is the position we are likely to be faced with in attempting a global consideration of moral behaviour, except that we are likely to be dealing with rather more than three factors, and it will therefore be difficult to construct an actual model within which we can physically represent relative placings. This means that, except for a small number of extreme cases, we cannot usefully attempt to differentiate between people by means of a single scale of moral goodness, but must rather take into account the different ways in which people may fail.

This multi-dimensional approach applies, too, to the question of the child's moral development. Many people, when considering this question, describe under the heading of moral development one important aspect, such as the child's moral thinking, the development of conscience, of social awareness and so on. These topics are, of course, important, but it is misleading to describe them in such a way that they let us believe we are dealing with the whole topic. In considering moral development, we need to know not only how the child's moral thinking changes, or how his conscience develops, but also about the development of his concern for other people, and of whatever abilities are necessary to express his concern and principles in action.

This leads us at once into a difficulty. Each of these things may be expected to grow in its own way, responding perhaps to factors which differ from each other. They do not perhaps function independently; the development of one may be expected to have a bearing on the development of the others. Clearly, we need to do what is always recommended in books on child development and take a global view rather than treat each one as though it existed in isolation. But this is likely to involve a degree of mental juggling of which the human mind is incapable. All we can usually manage is to look at the various dimensions of morality separately, while bearing in mind that there may exist a considerable degree of interaction.

This, in fact, will be the pattern followed in this book. We shall examine a few of the more important aspects of moral development, and, in the final chapter, go quickly over the material again, in order to suggest an overall developmental scheme.

SUMMARY

We cannot assign people to sharply-differentiated categories of morally good and morally bad. Nor can we place them along a single dimension of morality. There is evidence that a good deal of moral behaviour is specific to particular situations.

It is suggested that the most profitable approach is one which views moral behaviour as depending on a number of separate attributes, which may be regarded as orthogonal variables.

FURTHER READING

See Cattell (1), Eysenck (2, 4), Hartshorne (3), and Wilson (5).

3 Concern

There is a scene in Graham Greene's *The Third Man* which takes place in one of the cars of the Great Wheel in the Prater in post-war Vienna. Martins knows that Harry Lime's racket has been the black market sale of adulterated penicillin.

Martins said, 'Have you ever visited the children's hospital? Have you seen any of your victims?'

Harry took a look at the toy landscape below and came away from the door. 'I never feel quite safe in these things,' he said. He felt the back of the door with his hand, as though he were afraid that it might fly open and launch him into that iron-ribbed space. 'Victims?' he asked. 'Don't be melodramatic, Rollo. Look down there,' he went on, pointing through the window at the people moving like black flies at the base of the Wheel. 'Would you really feel any pity if one of those dots stopped moving – for ever? If I said you could have twenty thousand pounds for every dot that stops, would you really, old man, tell me to keep my money – without hesitation? Or would you calculate how many dots you could afford to spare? Free of income tax, old man. Free of income tax.' He gave his boyish conspiratorial smile. 'It's the only way to save nowadays.'

Some years earlier G. K. Chesterton had explored a similar idea in one of the Father Brown stories. *The Flying Hammer* is a short detective story, involving the solving of a murder in which the victim was brained by a hammer, though there was no one who could conceivably have been near enough to do it. At the end of the story it is discovered that the murder was committed by a demented vicar who sat at the top of the church tower and dropped the hammer on to the head of the person below as a physical manifestation of his moral judgement.

Both of these authors hit upon the idea of using height to symbolise someone's detachment or isolation from other human beings. When one looks down from a great height, everything, people included, assumes a less significant aspect. The people down below seem as though their reality is in some way diminished. In both of the examples we have quoted, however, we can go much further than this; the characters portrayed see other people as less important, not only when viewed from the top of the Great Wheel or the church tower, but all the time.

These two examples illustrate very clearly that component of moral behaviour which was described in the last chapter as PHIL. It is not so much a liking for other people, or any feeling of warmth for them, as a sense of their reality. Of course, the characters in the stories knew in one way that the people below were real, but when we say that the people were diminished in reality, we mean they ceased to matter, that their fates or feelings have become insignificant, that their rights as individuals, if they exist at all, are in some way less valid than one's own.

Nearly all Western systems of moral philosophy, whether religious or humanist in their orientation, have agreed that the central consideration for moral conduct is the effect of one's actions on other people. Implicit in this approach is the idea that people have equal rights. It is therefore possible to argue that this regard or concern for others, this feeling that they have a valid existence of their own, is a central feature of moral character. We reach the same conclusion if we look at the psychological evidence: those people in whom this characteristic is lacking seem to be deficient in many other departments of moral behaviour as well.

In this chapter, we shall discuss some of the evidence for regarding concern as a necessary condition for moral behaviour. We shall look at cases where it is deficient to discover the causes of this deficiency. These causes will lead us to form conclusions about the requirements for normal development in this direction. Finally, we shall look at other evidence from the field of child development.

DEPRIVATION

It is sometimes possible to use examples of abnormal development as a means of gaining information about the development of the normal personality. All that part of child development study which derives from psychoanalysis was built up in the first place on the basis of clinical evidence. There are dangers in such an approach, of course. Since we cannot usually tell in advance which people are going to require clinical treatment, work of this kind is usually retrospective. That is, it starts from the present disturbance and attempts to pick out circumstances in the patient's past history which may account for the trouble, and on this basis it may be possible to construct an account of how development has taken place. One of the difficulties with such a procedure is that it does not necessarily reveal how many normal people also experience at an earlier stage the thing that we have picked out as a causal factor. This is a very real difficulty, but clinical work can give us important leads, especially when there is a clear connection between the abnormal process being studied by the clinician and the particular aspect of normal behaviour which is the topic of the general psychologist. This is so in the present instance.

In the literature of criminology and delinquency, you will find frequent reference to a condition known as psychopathy. Unfortunately, the word is used, and misused, in a number of ways, but there is a particular disorder of personality described as the affectionless psychopath, the affectless child, or the 'frozen' child, about which there is considerable agreement. The most striking superficial features of the behaviour of this type of psychopath are his amoral and asocial qualities. Let us be quite clear that we are not talking simply about habitual criminals. The affectionless child is completely indifferent to the concept of morality, to the rules of society and to the needs and feelings of other people. He is equally without any sense of guilt. Naturally, it follows that he is frequently a persistent delinquent, but it does not follow that all persistent delinquents are psychopaths.

The affectionless psychopath can be regarded as the antithesis of the person of normal moral development, and for this reason a study of the condition may be expected to throw light on moral development. The deficiencies of the psychopathic personality correspond, as we shall see, to the abilities of the normal person. The psychopathic personality presents a negative picture of the dimensions of moral behaviour. This is the clear connection between the normal and the abnormal cases which was referred to above.

The topic has been studied by many psychologists over the past thirty years, and, though they frequently differ on points of detail, nearly all of them would agree with the following three points.

1. The affectionless psychopath shows a marked deficiency in emotional development, variously described as 'shallowness of affect', an inability to feel love, 'a curious inaccessibility infuriating to those trying to help'. He is unable to form lasting relationships with others, and has no friends in the normal sense of the word. Other people are merely means of satisfying his own needs. The reader will see at once the relationship between this characteristic and the component of moral behaviour which is the subject of this chapter; the point will be taken up again later.

2. He seems to be lacking in self-control. In this respect, his behaviour may be compared with that of pre-school children. We do not mean that he is necessarily a prey to every transient impulse: there may be considerations of expediency too obvious to be overlooked; the affectionless child tends to rely on such external control where the normal person relies on internal ones.

3. He lacks guilt feelings. This is perhaps the aspect which is most familiar to us through newspaper reports of psychopaths who have committed crimes which have attracted widespread attention. He is able to beat up an old age pensioner in order to steal a small amount of money without any feelings of remorse, or any regret for anything except for the fact that he himself has been caught and is getting into trouble.

Many people regard lack of guilt as being the main characteristic of psychopaths, but we shall see in the chapter on conscience that the first deficiency mentioned, the lack of capacity for relationships, is sufficient to account for the other two points. We can argue, then, that 'affectionless' is an apt description, since it refers to the salient feature of this disorder. We can argue, too, that there is a close connection between this capacity for emotional warmth and the aspect of moral behaviour which is the subject of this chapter. It is not that PHIL necessarily involves a warm relationship or a feeling of liking towards its object; it is rather that the existence of emotional ties with certain specific human beings influences our attitude towards more general classes of people. To say that we feel concern for the children in Africa who are suffering from malnutrition does not imply that we need to have feelings of warmth for them as we do for our friends. The evidence seems to show, however, that if we are incapable of forming emotional relationships with some people, we are not capable of feeling concern for anybody. Research done on the origins of the affectionless psychopathic state will therefore provide us with useful pointers to the origins of concern. The environmental deficiencies which cause the one show us the needs for the formation of the other.

The experiences which give rise to psychopathy take place in the first few years of life, long before the formation of conscience or the formulation of conscious moral values. This is why we may regard concern for others as being, not only conceptually but also in terms of actual development, central to the whole question of moral behaviour. It is, too, the reason why we are considering this topic before going on to look at those which are more explicitly concerned with morality.

The idea that deficiencies of a sort that we can call psychological or social could have serious effects on the development of the child was first reported as long ago as 1912. At that time, the usual outcome was death. It was reported, for instance, that there was one institution where no child who was admitted before the age of one year survived to the age of two. The physical conditions and the hygiene could not be faulted, and the cause therefore appeared to lie in the psychological or social conditions in which the child was placed. There is, in fact, a case on record where an impeccably hygienic and sterile institution was able habitually to bring about the recovery of ailing children by putting them in a foster home, that of an untidy, not very hygienic, but emotionally warm, coloured woman.

It appears that children who suffered such deprivation were

firstly abnormally susceptible to infection, particularly respiratory infection, and secondly that they had no drive to enable them to cope with this. Advances in medical treatment since that time have ensured that these appalling effects have disappeared; the child survives, as it were, whether he wants to or not. But more recent work has shown that a significant proportion of children brought up in institutional conditions have developed the character disorder described above.

At first, the culprit was thought to be the institution itself, and this in a sense was true, though, as we shall see, it is not sufficiently precise. The question which needed to be asked was: 'What is it about institutions which produce this particular effect?' A number of researchers and clinical workers gathered a body of evidence which pointed to maternal deprivation as being the chief cause. Rene Spitz, for instance, compared children of female criminals who were in the care of their own mothers in prison with children who had been placed in an orphanage. One would have said that all the physical and social conditions were in favour of the orphanage children, but in fact the children of the prisoners were more advanced developmentally. The only explanation which appeared to fit this was that the presence of the child's mother was the determining factor.

Observations of this kind were made over a number of years, and in 1951 John Bowlby published a report (6) for the World Health Organisation which formulated the problem very clearly and brought it to the concern of a much wider public. In this now very well-known work, he argued that the child needs a warm continuous relationship and that, if this is absent or broken, the child may develop the kind of character disorder we have been discussing. Two points should be noted. Although in normal circumstances this need will be met by the child's mother, who will be in any event more strongly motivated to meet the need than will anyone else, there is no absolute necessity for the relationship to be with the child's own biological mother. The child's need is for a particular relationship, not for a particular person. In cases where the family is broken through death or illness, the need can be met by a mother substitute, provided that this person is sufficiently motivated to behave towards the child as warmly and consistently as his own mother would have done.

We see now, then, that the institution was the culprit only insofar as it concentrated on physical rather than emotional needs. In a more recent research, Bowlby compared hospitalised and non-hospitalised children and concluded that it would be a mistake to think that institutionalisation necessarily or even commonly results in affectionless personality. As we have seen, the prime need is an emotional one, and, since nearly all institutions are now aware of the work which has been referred to here, conditions have been changed so as to permit the formation of the relationships which are necessary.

SENSORY STIMULATION

Not all psychologists, however, are agreed that talk about emotional deprivation is a sufficiently precise answer. Many argue that what is required is an optimum amount of sensory stimulation from the environment. This, too, fits the facts as we know them. The mother provides sensory stimulation by picking the baby up and cuddling him, talking to him – in addition to the routine activities of feeding and cleaning. The typical household, too, tends to provide a greater quantity and variety of sensory stimulation than does the old-fashioned institution; adults and children are coming and going; nearly everyone has a word for baby; and there is the radio and television. The emotional relationship, according to this view, is important in that it provides the mother with enough motivation to go on meeting the child's needs.

Experimental studies have tended to confirm the fact that sensory stimulation is important for the child's development (23). Of course, it is difficult to design experiments on this topic which are ethically acceptable. No one would contemplate nowadays submitting an experimental group of children to a possibly damaging deprivation in order to see if damage actually results from it. It has been possible to show, however, that babies who are given (under stringent experimental conditions which exclude the intrusion of other factors) short periods of sensory stimulation before a developmental test score significantly higher

c

than children in a control group who do not have this experience.

Perhaps we should pause to consider in passing the best-known experiment which leads to the opposite conclusion (23). Twin girls were raised to the age of about eight months in conditions of extreme isolation. That is, they were given no attention beyond that which was necessary for feeding and hygiene. At the end of this period their progress was compared with the norms for babies of their age in the population as a whole. No significant difference was reported. The experimenter concluded, on the basis of this work, that we carry out a great many actions in the bringing up of children which are not necessary. The trouble is, of course, that norms of this kind are essentially averages, and the attainments of the whole population at a given age shade away gradually on each side. In the absence of a control group, we are unable to say whether the girls in the experiment would have been *above* the norm if they had been brought up normally. One wonders why (granted that the experimenter can satisfy himself that the project is acceptable on ethical grounds) the twin girls were not subjected to different regimes, so that the effects of isolation could be measured as developmental differences between them. In view of these points, we cannot accept this experiment – widely quoted though it is in the textbooks – as serious evidence to set against more recent and carefully constructed work on the topic. We must conclude that it is clear that environmental stimulation does play a part in the development of the normal child.

What the experimenters have failed to show, on the whole, however, is that this form of deprivation is specifically related to a particular character disorder. Findings have generally been in terms of overall development, including intellectual and physical development, rather than in terms of specifically affective differences. We may distinguish, then, on the basis of the available evidence, two separate but intimately connected developmental needs: an adequate level of sensory stimulation which is necessary for the infant's general development (and there are, as we shall see in a later chapter, important connections between general and moral development) and a warm continuous relationship which is a prerequisite for the formation of that attitude of generalised concern for other people, which is itself a necessary component of all moral behaviour.

THE IDEA OF SELF

There is another approach to this problem, which need not involve us in conflict with what has already been said. This is to do with the child's development of a sense of self. The newly-born infant is equipped with a few innate behaviour patterns which are necessary for survival. These comprise responses like grasping and sucking and crying. There is little else that he can do. He cannot fixate objects with his eyes, he cannot direct the movements of his limbs. He has, as yet, no sense of identity, no perception of a boundary between 'me' and 'not me'. One of the first tasks of the earliest stage of infancy is the establishment of this boundary.

In part, of course, this is done at the level of sensory and motor activity. We have seen how stimulation from the environment impinges on the child's sensory system, and that this is related to developmental progress. In conjunction with this, the child explores his environment and his own body. At first, this is through unco-ordinated and random movements, but gradually physical control becomes established. The sense of self also develops in terms of the child's emotional life through the primary emotional relationship which is in normal circumstances with his mother. If this relationship is not established, we can argue that not only does the child lack a prototype for later attitudes of concern, but there is a diminishing at the emotional level of the child's very sense of himself as an identity. Such a reduction of his own validity necessarily implies a reduction in the validity of other people.

THE EGOCENTRIC PHASE

Many psychologists, when describing the development of children, find it useful to divide the child's growth into a sequence of phases. So that such phases are more than a collection of events which happen to be roughly contemporary with each other, developmental phases are frequently associated with the complementary ideas of developmental tasks and needs. The tasks may be regarded as the goals which a child must attain at a particular stage if he is to move on successfully. The needs may be regarded as what the environment must supply in order that these goals may be reached. An overall model of moral development which embodies this approach will be attempted in the final chapter. For the present, we can confine ourselves to those aspects of development which bear directly on the growth of concern.

Suppose that an infant has been successful in establishing this emergent sense of self. Can we say that this is a satisfactory conclusion to the matter? Clearly not, since the child still has the task of seeing what is the relationship between this self and the world around him, of building concepts which enable him to understand his place in his environment. For the very young child such relationships assume a completely different aspect from our own view of the world. This difference is often misunderstood – or not seen at all – by the adult, and yet it has a significant bearing on moral development.

The earliest phase of childhood is often described as *egocentric*. The word is used in its literal sense. The child sees himself as the centre of the world. All the activities of which he is aware seem to be carried out with reference to himself. This phase is also sometimes described as the *omnipotent* phase of infancy. The baby cries and, frequently, people appear to comfort or feed or clean him. He drops a toy; he is incapable of retrieving it himself, but someone else is usually on hand to pick it up for him, again and again until one or other tires of the activity. Not only is the infant the centre of the universe, but the universe exists entirely for his benefit.

The developmental goal of this phase is the enormous one of shifting the centre of the universe, a process which is sometimes described more prosaically as 'decentering'. The infant needs to learn that he is merely a self among other selves, that he is not omnipotent, that other people have needs and feelings, too. As an aspect of the child's emotional life, this process has been widely discussed in books on child development – particularly those with a psychoanalytic orientation. The process is worked out in terms of the emotional relationships between the child and the members of his family. He needs a great deal of emotional security, since he will only dare to move towards autonomy if he has a basically secure framework within which to operate. He has to acquire a basic sense of trust.

This shift in orientation is also bound up with the child's perception of the physical world. The child needs to be able to put himself in another person's place, and to appreciate that things look different from there. The abandonment of the ego-centric position may be traced in comparatively simple perceptual tasks, such as learning that the right and left hands of a person facing you are placed relative to that person, and not to yourself. Again, it is seen in the process of realising that what can be seen by a person on a step-ladder is not identical with your own view of the scene. In part, growth in this direction is brought about by development in the child's perceptual powers, which arises from the sensory and motor activities already discussed. If it is established that sensory stimulation has a bearing on the growth of concern, apart from its general developmental effects, this is the fashion in which we would expect it to work.

We see now how models or formulations in developmental psychology go some way towards tying together differing observations and theories about the nature and effects of depriva-tions in early childhood. They enable us, too, to formulate a sketch of the basic requirements for the development of concern: a stable and secure environment which provides an adequate level of sensory stimulation, adequate opportunity for the infant to explore this environment and, not least important, a warm continuous emotional relationship.

If we can draw up a pattern of phases of moral development which relates to the totality of moral behaviour rather than to one of its specific aspects, such as moral thought, we will place the development of PHIL at the beginning of this sequence. It is the first developmental goal on the road to moral maturity, and on its successful attainment depends a great deal of future growth in departments of behaviour which are not at first sight very obviously connected with it.

That is not to say that we can ignore this aspect of moral behaviour once the basic potentiality for concern has been established. This is one of the dangers which may arise from concerning ourselves too much with evidence based on pathological conditions. The difference between the normal and the abnormal may be so dramatic that we overlook the very great differences that may exist between normal individuals. Can we say that having concern is an absolute condition, like having brown eyes? Clearly not. Individuals differ, not only in the degree of concern which they experience, but also in the number of other people to whom they extend it. PHIL differs, then, in both intensity and range.

As far as differences in intensity are concerned, little that is useful can be said at present. It is perhaps tempting to relate this variable to the quality of the child's infantile experiences, but speculation of this kind is not really fruitful as a guide to bringing up children. It will be better to wait for evidence.

THE GENERALISATION OF CONCERN

Something can be said, however, about the development of concern if we restrict ourselves to talking about range. In a survey of moral thinking, sponsored by the Farmington Trust Research Unit, children were asked the following questions.

1. Which people do you think you ought to help?
2. Who else? (The interviewer continued prompting until the child either could offer no more instances, or brought the sequence to an end by making a general statement, such as 'Everyone'.)
3. Are there any people you needn't bother to help – it doesn't matter whether they get helped or not?
4. Are there any people whom it would be wrong to help?

The same sequence of questions was repeated with the concept of hurting substituted for helping: ('Which people is it wrong to hurt?' etc.).

The rationale behind these questions is fairly clear. Helping or hurting behaviour both have a clear relationship to the concept of PHIL. The range of individuals or classes of people who are to be helped, or who are not to be hurt, provides an indicator of the extent (but not the intensity) of the child's concern for others.

The children, whose ages ranged from four to eighteen, seemed in their answers to fall into the following categories, which may be taken as phases in the development of PHIL. As will be seen, these phases are characterised by growth in two directions, namely from the specific to the general, and from a proximity basis to a need basis; that is, from a basis of those individuals, or classes of individuals, whom the child happens to meet, to those whom the child perceives as being in need of particular attention.

1. The child extends his concern to a small number of specific, individually-named people. For the four-year-old these are, of course, members of his immediate family, plus, in some cases, a few adults whom he meets regularly – a grandmother who looks after him, the lady next door, and so on. As he gets older, the range is widened to include other children whom he plays with, or whom he meets in school, and his teacher. The number of named individuals can be quite large, without the basis for their selection being other than specific and proximity based.

2. The child becomes aware of individuals or limited classes of individuals who are particularly in need of help – babies, old people, crippled children. At this stage, although the concept of need is present and may represent a stronger tendency than the tendency to pick acquaintances, the child is still not capable of making full generalisations.

3. In the third phase, this generalisation has taken place, and we have answers like, 'Anybody who needs help', 'Anyone who is at a disadvantage compared with other people'. Answers of this kind were obtained from children at the top end of the primary school.

4. The pre-adolescent was typically able to generalise even more widely – 'You should help anyone who needs it; that's everybody, I suppose – we all need help sometime or other'. 'There isn't anyone who shouldn't be helped' (fully generalised if you work out the subject's complex negatives). 'You've got to help everybody'.

5. A small number of subjects, all of them adolescents, reached this further phase, which involves a more mature appreciation of the difficulties and conflicts which arise in putting such a general principle into practice. This was usually apparent in answers to

the last question, 'Are there any people whom it would be wrong to help?', to which answers such as the following were given: 'You should help everybody, even burglars and murderers – I don't mean you should help them commit a crime, but you've got to try and help them to be better.'

Those readers who are interested in Piaget's work on the development of the child's thinking (see chapter 5) may like to compare the above developmental phases with the Piagetian scheme.

PREJUDICE AND CONCERN

So far, in discussing the bearing of concern for others on the development of morality, we have tended to think about specific interpersonal decisions. The person who lacks PHIL is, we have seen, more likely to become delinquent, and is more prone to disregard the rights of others, both as regards their property and their persons. But it has a bearing, too, on public morality, on the wider issues of our time. Perhaps the most salient of these is the question of race relations. There is a clear connection between prejudice and concern, in particular the range of concern discussed in the preceding section. To be unprejudiced is simply to extend to people of other races that regard – PHIL, concern, acknowledgment of validity – which we extend to our family and friends. There are, of course, other factors involved, such as our tendency to come to conclusions as to matters of fact on the basis of a person's religion or colour, but if our PHIL is fully generalised, it would be perhaps difficult to do so.

There is a widely held view that prejudice is symptomatic not of some personality trait, like the restriction of the range of concern, but that it is simply a sign of ignorance about other races, an ignorance which arises in part through lack of social contact. According to this view, there would seem to be little need for specific moral education in this area, or need only for education of a factual sort, since prejudice may be expected to disappear as ignorance is diminished by contact – that if we simply hold things in check for a while, the problem will go away.

Unfortunately this does not seem to be supported by the

evidence. Recent work on the incidence of race prejudice in mixed and uni-racial communities shows that we cannot simply expect prejudice to disappear under the influence of wider acquaintance with the minority group. In fact, something like the reverse process seems to take place in many cases: prejudice is greater in mixed communities, liberalism more common in the absence of minorities. A study of voting patterns in a referendum held a few years ago in Australia powerfully illustrates this point. The referendum was on the question of whether the Aborigines should be entitled to full citizenship on an automatic rather than an earned or privileged basis. Nationally, the vote was overwhelmingly in favour of the reform, but detailed analysis showed a disquieting fact. The states were ranked according to two criteria: the percentage of votes cast in favour of the reform; and the percentage of the population which was aboriginal or part-aboriginal. A correlation was calculated between the two rank orders. This correlation was -0.9. That is, an almost perfect inverse relationship – the more Aborigines there were in a state, the greater the proportion of its citizens which would be likely to vote against reform.

Clearly, then, morality and equality in race relations cannot be left on a laissez-faire basis. They will not sort themselves out. The development of PHIL to its fullest extent provides an alternative, but we need information not only about the stages in its development, but also how they may be accelerated and consolidated.

CONCLUSION

The component of moral behaviour we have examined in this chapter has involved us in a wide range of considerations which serve to illustrate the fact that it is crucial to all forms of morality. It is, too, chronologically the earliest of the moral components. The evidence presented here goes some way towards illustrating the thesis that the pattern and quality of the care received by the infant in its earliest years may have a profound effect on attitudes in mature life which are both complex and important.

SUMMARY

The study of deprivation and of psychopathy suggests that the ability to feel concern for others, and, ultimately, to relate to some level, is crucial for moral development. This capacity is subject to developmental processes involving both intensity and generalisation, and is connected with such different later manifestations as conscience and race prejudice.

FURTHER READING

See Bowlby (6), Ainsworth (7), and Erikson (8).

4 Conscience

Two examples

Mary is five-years-old. Her mother is laying the table for tea, and puts a plate of chocolate biscuits on the table. Mary watches her mother go back to the kitchen. She looks at the biscuits, and then walks away to the other side of the room. She fixes her attention on the scene beyond the sitting-room window, but there is nothing much to look at in the garden and so it cannot compete with the lure of the chocolate biscuits. She keeps turning her head to look at them, and then, irresistibly drawn, she sneaks across the room, grabs a biscuit and crams it into her mouth. With bulging cheeks, she hurries back to the window, and swallows the biscuit with a speed which will give her indigestion if she tries to repeat the trick in a few years' time.

Presently she hears her mother's footsteps coming back from the kitchen. Appalled at the possible consequences, she sits rigid, staring at a blackbird on the lawn. All is well: the missing biscuit is not noticed, and mother goes back to the kitchen.

But presently Mary begins to show signs of a discomfort of another kind. She becomes restless, and the kitchen door seems to be exerting an attraction as strong as that of the plate of biscuits a short time ago. She approaches it several times, slowly, as though unwilling, and then stands in the doorway, waiting to be noticed. Her mother is too busy.

Red-faced, Mary speaks, 'Mummy, I just did something naughty . . .'

Here is another case: The scene is the interior of a small country church. A solitary tourist circumambulates the interior of the building, looking for points of architectural interest – perhaps rather aimlessly, since he is the sort of person who likes to be told what he ought to admire. He is about to leave the church, defeated, when he notices a pile of books on a table: 'A Brief History of the Church. Price 2/6.'

He picks up a copy, looks through it, and puts his hand into his pocket, only to find that he has no small change. He frowns in annoyance, then glances quickly around. There is still no one else in the building. He makes an incipient movement, as though about to put the book into an inside pocket. He hesitates. Finally, he shrugs, replaces the book on the pile, and goes outside.

THE MEANING OF 'CONSCIENCE'

In the preceding chapters, we have spent a great deal of time looking at various aspects of moral behaviour without so far giving very much thought to the idea of conscience, and yet for many people conscience is the crux of the matter. Morality is, in fact, frequently discussed as though conscience were the only consideration, a point of view which leads to the conclusion that all important moral values are acquired in the first few years of life, and that there is very little we can do about a child's moral development after that time. Nowadays, we tend to associate this viewpoint with the psychoanalytic concept of the superego, but it is in fact, in one form or another, a much older idea than that. It was, after all, the Jesuit educators who used to say that if they had the care of a child until he was seven, they would not worry about him for the rest of his life.

As we have seen, it can be argued that the equation of conscience with morality is an oversimplification, and an unjustified narrowing of the latter concept. The argument can be pressed further – to the conclusion that such an equation arises from a serious *misuse* of the word 'morality'. Such arguments are to do with evaluative uses of the word 'moral', of course. They do not imply that conscience is not an important factor to be taken into account when describing the child's moral development.

As is so often the case, we must begin by looking at the meaning of the word. 'Conscience' is a term which presents a number of concealed difficulties. Most people use it with complete confidence, as though its meaning is self-evident. But, in fact, the word is used in a number of different ways. Some theologians talk as though conscience were a divinely implanted entity which necessarily reveals an absolute moral law. Psychologists regard it as being a pattern of value judgements, which is related to the values of the parents and the way in which the child has been brought up. Even in everyday speech, we use the word in different ways. 'A guilty conscience' implies something which arouses feelings of guilt *after* we have done something wrong; 'your conscience tells you . . .' implies the existence of something which warns us *in advance* that something or other should not be done.

The first difficulty, then, is that, since we use one word in all these different ways, we may be led to conclude that we are dealing with a single phenomenon. A second, related difficulty is that we tend to reify concepts like conscience. It is very easy to fall into this trap, since we frequently use the word transitively, as when we say, 'His conscience stopped him . . .' or 'His conscience troubled him'. And we do not necessarily avoid the difficulty by using a technical term such as 'superego'. Our ideas are perhaps not so naïve that we actually imagine a *homunculus* living somewhere inside us, passing judgements on what we do, but our habits of thought are not necessarily as far removed from this as might at first sight appear. The point is that we are actually talking about patterns of response, or of behaviour, which form a recognisable, coherent and probably permanent part of the individual's psychological organisation.

The next point is that we must distinguish between the main usages of the word. Probably the most important distinction is the one which is already implied above in the two examples quoted of our everyday use of the word. It is surprising that this distinction has existed all along in our day-to-day speech (though it has been implicit rather than explicit), while it has only recently made its appearance in the more technical literature of the subject. We must distinguish, then, between conscience as an advance warning, and as an arouser of guilt after the act.

The first of these we may regard as being the inhibitory aspect of conscience, or as a non-rational conviction that certain things are right or wrong. The word 'non-rational' may cause difficulty We do not mean that it is *irrational* in the sense of being unreasonable; what we are talking about is, rather, the method by which the conclusion is arrived at. That stealing is wrong is an entirely reasonable belief, but people may hold it non-rationally, or, if you prefer, they may know it intuitively.

This is something which we must all have experienced. Beliefs of this kind are often clung to, even when all the reasons seem to point in another direction. We may be presented with a very carefully reasoned argument, which purports to show that there is nothing really wrong in obtaining more income tax allowances than we are entitled to, or travelling on a train without a ticket. Even though we may be for the moment unable to answer this argument properly, in the sense of being able to demonstrate an error in it, we nevertheless retain a strong feeling that, in spite of the arguments, it is just a wrong thing to do. Not everyone's conscience is the same, of course. The reader may be quite willing to accept arguments in favour of doing the things mentioned above, but there are almost certainly other topics on which he brings these non-rational judgements to bear.

Again, we may look at this inhibitory aspect of conscience as being something which governs our moral behaviour, even when we are alone. Put yourself in the place of the tourist in the example at the beginning of the chapter. Or imagine yourself to be buying a newspaper from one of those coin-box stands. Most people probably could not bring themselves to take the book, or a paper, without paying, even if they were in a completely deserted building or street. It is not that they are afraid of being caught, nor that they have worked out that they would feel guilty afterwards, but that they have a strong intuitive feeling that it must not be done.

The second main usage of the word is to do with the experience of guilt. We do something wrong, and we are afterwards troubled with a guilty conscience. Insofar as this becomes a motive which influences our behaviour *before* the act, this is quite clearly a much more rational proceeding than the aspect we have just been discussing. But the experience of guilt itself is by no means a rational matter. Guilt is not experienced in proportion to the importance of the misdemeanour. It differs between people: some people commit the most terrible crimes with no feelings of guilt, while others feel guilty over the slightest fault. Indeed, some of the people who suffer pangs of guilt most strongly are those who lead the most exemplary lives. Freud even suggested that the experience of guilt is inversely proportionate to wickedness. It is also true that there are variations within the same individual. We are not consistent in the intensity of guilt we experience for different kinds of wrong actions, and indeed we may sometimes feel guilty for no reason at all. This often tends to happen when we are faced by someone in a position of authority. Children often show signs of guilt when the headmaster talks at assembly about a breach of the school rules, even when this has been done by some other child. People often feel inappropriate or irrational guilt when they are faced with a customs officer, even though their baggage contains not so much as a single cigarette over the allowance.

We have said enough to demonstrate that it is possible to make a conceptual distinction between two uses of the word 'conscience'. Is there any evidence that this distinction exists, too, at the level of actual behaviour? The traditional view is, as we have seen, that which is implied by the use of a single word for the two aspects, namely that both are produced by the same agency. This would lead us to suppose that the two things are correlated, that the person who has the strongest inhibition against doing some wrong thing is the one who feels most guilty if he succumbs to temptation and does it.

Now we can certainly think of cases where these two aspects of conscience are uncorrelated. There are many alcoholics, for instance, who suffer agonies of guilt over the effects of their addiction on their families, but who are nevertheless quite incapable of resisting the temptation to get drunk. And we need not depend on extreme examples of this kind. We all know students who feel genuinely guilty about persistently missing nine o'clock lectures, and who are nevertheless unable to get out of bed in the mornings in time to do anything about it.

Solomon carried out an interesting experiment which illustrates this point (4, 5). His experiment was concerned with different ways of training puppies. We know, of course, that prohibitions taught to dogs are not the same thing as moral behaviour, and that we must be careful whenever we try to transfer findings which relate to simple animals to more complex animals. Nevertheless, the experiment demonstrates how, at a simple level, the kind of distinction we have in mind may be manifested in actual behaviour. It gives us a lead, too, about the way these two patterns of behaviour may originate.

The training task was a simple one. The puppies were taught that it was 'wrong' to eat fresh horsemeat and 'right' to eat patent dogfood out of a can. (Don't believe everything they tell you on the television – the puppies preferred the fresh horsemeat.) The training method was the ordinary one used by many pet owners: the puppy was tapped with a newspaper for committing a prohibited act. Two very slightly differing training methods were used. Some of the puppies were punished for approaching the wrong plate, and others were punished after they had eaten some of the horsemeat. Thus, the important difference in the training was the timing of the punishment – whether it occurred before or after the prohibited act.

The puppies were then, when hungry, taken into a room (one at a time) in which there was a plate of horsemeat in the middle of the floor, but none of the permitted food. They were apparently unsupervised, but the experimenter was able to observe them from a concealed point outside the room. The puppies were thus put into a situation analogous to being faced with a temptation.

Two observations emerged from this experiment. Firstly, there was a wide range of difference in the length of time which elapsed before a puppy abandoned its training and ate the meat. Some of them lasted out for a few minutes only, but one of them fasted for more than a fortnight before the experiment was stopped. These differences may lead us to suppose that there may be a constitutional factor involved, since they did not correspond to differences in training method.

The second observation arose from the next phase of the experiment, when the experimenter had come into the room. Two opposing patterns of behaviour were distinguished. Some of the puppies had shown every sign of apprehension before eating the meat, but once they had given in to the temptation, they gave no sign of disturbance at all. On the contrary, they were pleased to see the experimenter when he came back into the room, greeting him with wagging tails.

Others – which had usually had a much lower temptation resistance (measured by the length of time which elapsed before the meat was eaten) – became very disturbed after they had eaten the meat, and when the experimenter came in, they would slink away with their tails between their legs, and try to avoid him.

These two response patterns – the inhibitory response and the guilt response – were found to be related to the timing of the administration of punishment. Punishment administered before the meat had been eaten led to inhibition; if it was delayed until afterwards, a guilt response was found instead.

We shall see presently that a simple reward and punishment model cannot be applied in a straightforward fashion to the development of conscience in human beings. Nevertheless, the experiment seems to demonstrate that the distinction we have made on conceptual grounds may not only appear in actual behaviour, but also arise from differences in training patterns.

The distinction has been sustained again in a more recent research, and one which deals directly with children's moral thinking. This research will be dealt with more fully in chapter 6, but one point which relates to our present discussion is that the children's responses often showed very clear distinctions between conscience as inhibition ('It just is right'; 'It doesn't have to have a reason'; 'No one told me – I just know it'; 'My own brains told me') and conscience as guilt ('I'd feel terrible whenever I re-membered it'; 'If I did that, I'd feel all funny inside'; 'I couldn't get it out of my mind'). The eleven-year-old group in the sample (eighty children) were scored according to the frequencies with which they gave each type of response. Although forty-nine of them responded in terms of either both aspects of conscience, or neither, there were thirty-one who responded in one way, but not the other. We are dealing, in fact, with another example of low positive correlation, such as was discussed in chapter 2.

D

To sum up what has been said in the first part of this chapter, we may distinguish between conscience as a non-rational or intuitive feeling of right and wrong, and conscience as the experience of guilt. Although guilt, too, is not apparently the result of a rational process, some element of causal thinking must be involved whenever guilt becomes a reason for behaviour considered in advance of a wrong act. There is an obvious difference, even in the absence of the first type of conscience, between the person who reasons, 'If I do that, I'll feel guilty, therefore I won't do it', and the person who does not look ahead in this way, and finds his guilt feelings lying, as it were, in ambush.

THE ORIGINS OF CONSCIENCE

We must turn now to the question of how conscience originates. We have already seen that the distinction we have just been discussing has not usually been made in most of the literature on the subject, and we must therefore make up our own minds in each case which aspect of conscience is being referred to. We shall look at some of the theories and some of the evidence relevant to the topic and then, in summing them up, relate them to the foregoing discussion.

The simplest explanation is probably that conscience is the result of parental rewards and punishments. This is the assumption which lies behind a great deal of the things parents do, and the experiment with the puppies, described earlier, may incline us to believe that it plays an important part. It appears, however, that the matter is not so simple.

In an experiment carried out before the war, MacKinnon gave ninety-three subjects a number of problems to solve, with an opportunity to cheat to get the answers. They did not know that they were under observation through a one-way screen, and the experimenter was able to identify which of them cheated (about half of the subjects). Some time later they were interviewed to discover whether they would admit cheating, and whether they felt guilty about it. Those who denied cheating (whether truly or not) were asked whether cheating *would* have made them feel guilty. Only a quarter of those who had cheated said they had felt, or would have felt, guilty, whereas over eighty per cent of the non-cheaters thought they would have experienced guilt. So far, however, the experiment has only demonstrated an inverse relationship between guilt and honesty. But some time later, MacKinnon carried out an enquiry into the kind of training his subjects had received as children. Although this part of the survey only covered part of the original sample, the results are of considerable interest. Over three-quarters of the cheaters recalled physical punishments, as opposed to less than half of the non-cheaters. On the other hand, 'psychological punishments' were recalled by over half of the non-cheaters, and less than a quarter of the cheaters. Similar findings have been reported by more recent studies. Sears, Maccoby and Levin interviewed nearly 400 mothers, to obtain information about the disciplinary techniques they used and the behaviour of their children (15). The interviews were constructed in such a way as to obtain indirect ratings of the strength of the child's conscience. This survey confirmed MacKinnon's findings. Only fifteen per cent of the children whose parents used physical punishments had strong consciences; where the parents made little use of physical punishment, the proportion of children with strong consciences was twice as great.

Again, a number of studies on aggressive behaviour in children have shown that where children are given physical punishments to stop them being aggressive, the result is usually a more than average aggressive child.

As far as reward and punishment is concerned, then, the important thing for the formation of conscience appears to be not the severity of the punishment, but its nature. Or perhaps we should put it another way: for the young child, the severity of the punishment is not to be measured in terms of whether or not it is corporal punishment, but in terms of whether the child feels he has temporarily lost his parent's approval and love. This fits in with another of the findings of the Sears' study, namely that those mothers who were rated as having a warm attitude towards their children were also more likely to have children with strong consciences.

The possible connection between the child's feeling of loss of love and the growth of conscience brings us to the next theoretical approach. This is the approach associated particularly with Freud and the psychoanalysts. In this context, the term we meet is 'superego'. This, of course, is part of the psychoanalytic model of the structure of personality, according to which human behaviour can be discussed in terms of the interaction between the three 'institutions' of the personality: the *id*, which is concerned with obtaining instinctual gratification; the superego, which approximates to what we have described here as the guilt aspect of conscience; and the ego, which is the rational, reality-oriented part of the mind, mediating between the other two and the environment.

Freud describes the formation of the superego in terms of *introjection*. We must make it clear at the outset that the use of the technical term of this kind does not imply – and is not intended to imply – knowledge of the actual means by which the process is accomplished. The word refers to the incorporation into one's own personality of some aspect of another. We usually think of this as happening in the context of the acquisition of moral values and guilt responses by young children.

The best known Freudian formulation was connected with the idea of the Oedipus complex. The child's attachment to the parent of the opposite sex and jealousy of the parent of the same sex result, it was said, in an emotional crisis. The child has to give up the exclusiveness of this attachment, and at this point he introjects aspects of the love object he has given up.

Most psychologists would now regard an attempt to connect the formation of conscience so exclusively with a particular emotional crisis as being unnecessarily restrictive, but in drawing attention to the connection between superego formation and the feared loss of love, Freud has put forward an idea which, as we have seen, has survived the test of more empirical surveys.

But this was not the only contribution of the psychoanalysts. An alternative (or supplementary) formulation was proposed by Anna Freud (14). According to this, the child identifies with the object of fear. If another person (such as an angry person) is seen by the young child as being threatening, a possible defensive reaction is to identify with the threatening figure. Again, we are dealing with a suggestion based upon purely clinical evidence, which has echoes in more empirical work, which will be described below.

But why, you may ask, do we invoke such sophisticated explanations? Would it not be sufficient to say that young children tend to imitate their parents? Though this may provide us with an answer, for we know that children are great mimics, it cannot provide us with the whole answer. If it were the only factor involved, children's behaviour would always resemble that of their parents, and we know from everyday observation that this is not so. Clearly, if the idea of imitation is to take us any further forward, we need to know which aspects of a parent are likely to be imitated. Some of the work already quoted may give us a clue to this. We have seen that when parents beat their children to stop them from being aggressive, they are likely to produce aggressive children. We remember, too, Anna Freud's suggestion about identification with the object of fear. A parent who beats his child may be said to act aggressively, and the observation about the child's behaviour thus appears to make sense. In this connection, too, we can quote a number of experiments aimed at finding out what kind of people a child imitates. Bandura and Ross, in experiments in which a child was given the opportunity to imitate various kinds of people, showed that social power was the chief determinant. The subject, for instance, saw one figure who was the possessor of a large collection of toys, and another who was given the toys to play with. The first is in a position of social power; the second in a position which may be envied for other reasons. The children mainly imitated the figure with social power.

It seems, then, that there is no single factor which can account for the development of conscience. Probably each of the processes described above contributes in its own way to the formation of a different aspect of conscience, and here we must return to our earlier distinction between conscience as a guilt arouser and as an intuitive or irrational moral judgement.

1. We have seen that reward and punishment can, in certain circumstances, produce both guilt and inhibition, and that

the factor which seems to determine whether it is the one or the other is the timing – whether incipient or actual transgressions are punished. Processes of this kind may often operate as classical conditioning; an organised pattern of conditioned aversions does seem to provide an economic explanation of the intuitive aspect of conscience. This explanation has certain limitations, however, and – particularly for the guilt response – psychological punishments, like loss of love, are the more effective; conscience therefore seems to develop best within an emotionally warm environment.

2. Explanations involving introjection seem to relate mainly to the guilt aspect. These approaches can be reconciled with some of the foregoing findings.

3. Imitation appears to account for the intuitive or control aspects, and children tend to imitate people with social power.

We have already had reason to notice the discrepancy between the intentions of moral training and the type of values which are acquired by the child. Parents, you will remember, who used physical punishments to discourage aggressive behaviour, tended to produce aggressive children. This underlines the fact that the formation of conscience is something which goes on not only in a rather complex fashion, but also below the level of rationality. Where moral education is seen as merely a matter of implanting a conscience in either sense of the word, deliberately worked out programmes may be extremely unpredictable, since we cannot always be sure which of the many possible mechanisms we are activating. Beating a child for being aggressive is presumably based on a reward and punishment rationale: the resulting behaviour is apparently based on imitation of a powerful adult, or identification with the object of fear. If the punishment is administered after the aggressive act, we cannot rule out the possibility that there will be little inhibition of aggressive behaviour, coupled with guilt feelings about it when it is indulged in.

Everything that has been said up to now points to a relationship between the values acquired by the child and the values of the parent. But this relationship, too, needs examining rather more closely. It must be clear by now that we are not necessarily dealing with parental values as consciously expressed. The child is far more strongly influenced by the actual values of the parent. This is strikingly true where imitation is the operative mechanism, but it applies to other cases as well. We have seen that one of the most powerful determinants is disapproval or loss of love. There is little point in refraining from punishing a child for some trivial accident, such as breaking a cup, if our tightly controlled anger and disapproval are visible in every rigid muscle. Freud has suggested that the superego of the child is related to the superego of the parent.

CONSCIENCE AND CULTURE

We have been discussing conscience so far as though it were a universal concept. But are we entitled to make this assumption? Obviously, at the least, we must make certain limitations. Not everyone's conscience is of equal strength, and we have seen in the previous chapter that psychopaths seem to be devoid of conscience altogether. But there is more to this question than a matter of *individual* variation. Riesman suggested that we can distinguish between other-directed and inner-directed individuals. The latter tend to govern their behaviour by means of internal controls, and transgression is associated with guilt. Other-directed individuals tend to be governed more by the expectations of other people, and in this case the emotion associated with transgression is referred to as shame. (Ordinary speech does not always follow this particular usage. We may say, 'I was ashamed of myself' when we mean 'I felt guilty'.) The other-directed person relies, like Pinocchio, on an external conscience, and his behaviour is less predictable when he is unobserved, or unlikely to be caught out. Riesman raised the interesting point that these differences characterise not only different individuals within a single culture, but also different cultures. Western societies have tended to be inner-directed, while Japan is often quoted as an example of an other-directed society. This distinction makes a great deal of sense. It fits in with the importance of the idea of 'loss of face' in many Oriental societies.

It was argued, too, that many Western societies are in a stage of transition, that we are moving away from inner-direction towards other-direction. If we look at the value systems which have been ascribed to contemporary surburban life, with its emphasis on conformity and keeping up with the Jones, this suggestion, too, seems a plausible one. But it may be that it is less plausible now than when the argument was first advanced. It is equally plausible (but by no means proved) that the present aggressive non-conformity and concern with certain moral values among young people today indicates a return to an older approach to moral thinking, which emphasises individual conscience.

We must be cautious, then, in any cross-cultural application of the idea of conscience – a point which is particularly important in those societies which have a large population of recently arrived immigrant children. But are we entitled, as some people have done, to press this to its limit and claim that people in some societies have no conscience at all? MacIntyre has implied that this is the case. It is not without significance, he has argued, that the classical world has no word equivalent to our word 'conscience'. To argue about the objective existence of the phenomenon in terms of whether people have formulated a concept which corresponds to it seems a doubtful procedure. It is said that certain tribes of Eskimos have no word for snow; and the autonomic nervous system did not wait to put in an appearance until we had a word for it. As we have seen, the word which we do have for it in our society by no means corresponds exactly to the observed phenomena.

If we glance back at the mechanisms which may be involved in formation of conscience, we find that it is difficult to imagine that most of them are restricted to members of a given culture. The introjection of *parental* values certainly may be culture-bound; we cannot say very much about this, since it relates to an inter-personal process rather than to a clearly understood mechanism. It seems improbable, however, that conditioning, the effect of reward and punishment, and similar factors, are culturally specific. Nor does it seem likely that children in other cultures never imitate their elders (though, of course, in these cases it may well be that social power is not the determinant).

It is probably better to say, in spite of the fact that on this occasion the Greeks did not have a word for it, that those aspects of conscience which depend on fairly simple and universal behavioural characteristics are probably universally present, but that, in certain cultures, where inner-direction is not so highly valued as a method of making moral judgements, this type of control is less esteemed and plays a very much smaller part in determining behaviour.

To sum up, we are now able to build the following picture of conscience.

1. It may be regarded as two phenomena: inhibition or control, and guilt arousal.
2. It is not amenable to conscious control.
3. A number of processes may contribute to the formation of different aspects of conscience. Among these are intro-jection, reward and punishment, imitation.
4. It is based in the first instance upon actual parental attitudes rather than parental teachings.
5. It is variable as between individuals and in between cultures.
6. Where it exists, it is a relatively permanent feature of the individual's mental organisation.

Conscience is only one of a number of factors which determine human behaviour when one is confronted with a moral problem, but, compared with some other determinants, such as the ability to formulate moral judgements, it is remarkably reliable and consistent. It may be that guilt and non-rational inhibition are the most frequent governors of actual behaviour, at least in our society. This, however, does not entitle us to equate concepts of conscience with moral behaviour when we use the word 'moral' in its evaluative sense. No matter how closely conscience is con-nected with (descriptively) moral development, if we evaluate behaviour as moral insofar as it implies responsibility for the consequences of our actions, its very non-rationality must dis-qualify it as moral behaviour in the fullest sense of that term.

It follows from this that our account of moral development must be extended to include other facets of behaviour, which will be discussed below.

THE IDEAL SELF

So far, this chapter has emphasised the negative, or prohibitory, aspects of moral behaviour, as though morality were chiefly a matter of not doing certain things which are wrong, rather than of doing things that are right. Since we have been concerned to a great extent with the evidence available, this emphasis reflects the trend of the experimental work which has been carried out; and this, in turn, perhaps, reflects a more widespread, and a more ancient, public orientation to the topic – the Ten Commandments, after all, exhibit a similar prohibitory inclination.

'Negative' instances are useful, too, because they frequently provide more specific and clear-cut examples with which to illustrate the underlying psychological principles. It would, however, be wrong to move on from the aspects of the subject discussed in this chapter without taking a look at a more positive instance.

In a previous chapter, we discussed the development of the sense of self. It would be possible to elaborate this idea into a set of fine distinctions – the self-image, the body image, the ideal self, and so on – which would rival those of the medieval theologian, but it is fortunately possible to concentrate for our present purposes on one of these, the ideal self. We can regard this, as the name suggests, as an idealised version of the self – a kind of internalised exemplar, representing ourselves as we would like to be, against which our behaviour, both actual and prospective, can be assessed. It is not so much a question of explicitly formulating a question ('Am I the sort of person to do such a thing?'), though this can happen, as having, as it were, a picture of an ideal self, which influences decision, sometimes at a level which is barely conscious.

The ego-ideal is included in a chapter on conscience for obvious reasons: the acquisition of this system of values resembles, in many respects, the processes which have been described above, and, for this reason, it will not be discussed again. The reader's attention is directed especially to the work on introjection and on imitation; it would be tedious to repeat the material.

In discussions on moral behaviour, the possession of 'high ideals' is usually reckoned to be a key criterion, and, of course, there is a sense in which this is true. At the same time, however, we should be aware of the dangers and limitations involved with this basis for moral action.

An unrealistic level of aspiration can be self-defeating. This can perhaps be most clearly illustrated by reference to another aspect of behaviour, that of career aspirations. These, too, can provide considerable motivation, but when unrelated to the individual's actual capacities, they are discouraging and self-defeating. To wish to become a policeman, or a judge, or an air-line pilot are all laudable ambitions, but if the person whose ambitions they are is of below-average height, or incapable of analysing abstract arguments, or extremely short-sighted, all his efforts are being directed into an unproductive channel; he will, in many cases, achieve less than someone whose aspirations were more modest, but more realistic. Similarly with moral behaviour: if there is no recognisable relationship between the ideal and the actual self, what may emerge is a disabling degree of guilt, and, in extreme cases, total withdrawal.

If the ego-ideal should relate to the real self, then it follows that it must have some capacity for adaptation. In the course of his development, a child has to come to grips with some extensive emotional and physical reorganisations, the most striking of which is perhaps adolescence. Changes in the body (and the body-image), the emergence of new propensities, these cannot be assessed in terms of an ego-ideal which is fixated at an infantile level.

Another difficulty is that certain aspects of the ideal self may not relate to morality at all. A recent enquiry into the question of smoking and schoolchildren illustrates this. It appeared that one of the main motivations for smoking was that the habit was associated with, or symbolised, character traits which were valued by children who smoked – they were related, in other words, to the child's ego-ideal. These traits were all connected with such ideas as toughness or virility, ideas which have no necessary relationship with morality: if anything, they may have a slight negative correlation with moral behaviour.

And, of course, there may be cases where we are dealing with ideals which are not simply irrelevant to morality, but which are opposed to it. Where a child has been brought up in a delinquent sub-culture, even normal processes of imitation or introjection can result in the emergence of perverted ideals. Something of this sort happened on a national scale in pre-war Germany.

CONCLUSION

Both conscience and ideals, then, have similar limitations as motives for moral behaviour. While it cannot be denied that they furnish powerful – and probably the commonest – behaviour controls, they may function at a level which is far removed from the ideas of rationality and responsibility. Both have their foundations laid when the child is far too young to have any understanding of the moral issues involved, and both can be perverted to immoral ends.

An interesting and important legal case, turning in part on this point, is currently being brought in the United States. A young man, who was under twenty-one, refused, on grounds of conscience, in common with many others, to register for military service, since this would involve him in – at the very least – giving implicit support to the Viet Nam war. He was convicted under the draft laws and sentenced to a term of imprisonment. His mother appealed against this sentence. One of the grounds for this appeal was that, since the mother, and not the son, is responsible for his ideals and the nature of his conscience, it should be the mother, not the son, who suffers any legal penalty which is incurred for reasons of conflict.

This would not be the place to pursue this argument, but it may well prove an interesting and worthwhile exercise for the reader to discuss the extent to which such a claim is justified by the evidence on the nature and origin of conscience presented in these pages.

SUMMARY

Two aspects of conscience were distinguished: the inhibitory and the guilt arousing. Experimental work relates these to different patterns of conditioning. Conscience cannot be accounted for in terms of a single causal factor, such as aversive conditioning, punishment or imitation, and it is likely that each of these plays a part in its development.

FURTHER READING

See Eysenck (4), Brown (9), Stephenson (10), Aronfreed (11), Flugel (12), Freud (13), and Anna Freud (14).

5 Moral Judgement

One day in the middle of winter, there was snow on the ground and the village pond was frozen hard. Johnnie Green didn't want to go to Sunday School; he wanted to go skating instead. He knew that if he asked his parents, they would not give him permission to stay away, so he hid his skates under his jacket, and, holding his Bible in his hand, where everyone could see it, he set out. Once he was out of sight of the house, he ran to the pond for an afternoon's skating. But the ice was not as thick as it looked, and when he got to the middle it cracked, and he fell down into the dark water. Everyone was at Sunday School, and so no one heard his cries for help. They carried his body home about tea-time.

If Johnnie had been a good boy, and gone to Sunday School as he should, this would never have happened to him.

This Victorian moral tale for children embodies one kind of moral judgement – or perhaps two kinds, since the boy's fate was, its author would have no doubt said, 'a judgement on him'. Compare the moral thinking in the story with that in the following shorter quotations:

He never wants anything but what's right and fair; only – when you come to settle what's right and fair, it's everything that he wants and nothing that you want.

(Hughes: *Tom Brown's Schooldays*)

Habit with him was the test of truth,
'It must be right: I've done it from my youth.'
(Crabbe: *The Vicar*)

The differences which can be seen in these quotations are concerned with the basis for moral judgements, and it is with differences of this kind that we will be concerned in this chapter.

Bases for moral judgements

We must distinguish the development of moral thinking from the development of values. In the latter case, we are saying that a person believes this to be wrong at one age, and that to be wrong when he is a little older and so on. In considering a person's moral thought, we are more concerned with the means by which a conclusion is reached. Many people may agree that stealing is wrong, but whereas one person may base his belief on deference to the law, another may base it on an unthinking regard for his own conscience. One person may be concerned with conforming to the norms of his society, another may produce arguments about the *effect* of stealing upon that society. Such different bases for making judgements imply very different ways of thinking about right and wrong.

But why, it might be argued, do these differences matter? Surely, you may argue, it is *what* a person believes rather than *why* he believes it which is important. And to this argument may be added the results of various objective enquiries which show that the correlation between moral thinking and moral behaviour is not very high.

There are a number of reasons why the topic is important. Admittedly, it is better that people in general do the (descriptively) moral thing for whatever reason than that they do not do it at all. It is better that people refrain from murdering each other for the not very (evaluatively) moral reason that they are scared of the punishment than that murder and mayhem prevail. But in describing moral development, we are doing more than merely listing those forms of behaviour which may be good for society. If we regard morality as being linked in some way with the notion of responsibility, then we are bound to distinguish between, for instance, the person who refrains from murder because he understands the principles involved, and the one who responds to aversive conditioning in childhood.

Secondly, we can argue that some modes of thought are linked more reliably to acceptable values and behaviour than others. European history during the middle years of this century has shown us, for instance, the deplorable consequences which can arise from linking the idea of morality too closely with that of obedience.

Thirdly, to turn to the evidence from psychological surveys, the low correlations found in such studies as the Hartshorne and May work, described in an earlier chapter, need not, if interpreted correctly, lead us to too pessimistic a conclusion about the part played by moral thinking. The correlations were all positive, and the relationship was generally significant. The same point of interpretation was discussed in an earlier chapter: a person's behaviour is in agreement with his moral judgements more than half the time – if it were 50/50, the correlation would be zero, and a negative correlation would indicate agreement between moral thinking and behaviour on less than half of the occasions. Admittedly, the findings show that there are a great many occasions when the two are not in accord. But is not this what we would predict? We have seen that morality is, from the psychologist's point of view, a matter of a great number of interacting factors within any one individual. Moral thinking is only one of these. In addition, an individual's behaviour is influenced by a great many other factors, which are not concerned with morality at all – aesthetic, self-seeking, sexual, and so on. And when we talk in this context about a person's moral beliefs, it must be remembered that we are actually referring to the person's moral thinking as portrayed by some research instrument – a questionnaire, an interview or an essay. None of these gives an entirely pure measure, the subject's answers being contaminated by a combination of extraneous factors which is peculiar to each instrument. These may include such diverse things as the subject's desire to create a good impression; in written tests, his intelligence and verbal ability; in questionnaires, his tendency to agree or disagree consistently with whatever is written down. When we consider the number of intervening factors, we should perhaps be surprised not that the correlations are so low but that they manage to attain a level significantly greater than zero. The correct interpretation of such findings, then, is that they are entirely consistent with a view that moral thinking and moral judgement have a part to play in actual behaviour.

DEVELOPMENTAL PATTERNS

We must begin by making sure that we understand what we have in mind when we talk about the development of thinking. It is clear that more is involved than simply listing the thoughts and beliefs which typify children of different ages. A developmental scheme must analyse in some way the thought processes involved, and it must *relate* them chronologically rather than simply *list* them in chronological order. That is, they should go some way towards showing us how one pattern of behaviour arises from its predecessor. Usually, such an analysis involves classifying the kind of concept of which children at different levels of development are capable, or analysing the kinds of mental operations which they can carry out. Such analyses will normally lead to an overall picture in the form of a sequence of phases or stages.

A sequence of phases seems a straightforward idea, but in fact it can refer to a number of rather different situations.

1. *Consecutive phases*

In a sequence of this kind, the phases follow each other in a definite order, and, as each phase is attained, the preceding one is left behind. It is as if the child were passing through a suite of rooms. He has to go through the first room in order to reach the second, and he cannot be in two rooms at once. Perhaps the clearest example of such a sequence can be found outside our present topic and in the physiological development of sex. A rough division into phases for the years between eight and twenty might be: pre-pubescent; pubescent; adolescent; sexually mature. We know that the sequence must be passed through in a definite and invariable order; that the process is irreversible – having become adolescent, you cannot return to the pre-pubertal stage; and that it is impossible to be in two stages at once. It has sometimes been held that a similar developmental model may be applied to the development of thinking in general and to moral thinking in particular, but we shall discuss this possibility in more detail later in the chapter.

2. *Cumulative phases*

It is also possible, however, that the attainment of one stage does not preclude the continuation of operations at the previous

E

one, so that we have a cumulative sequence in which each new pattern is added to what has gone before. The development of communication gives us a fairly clear illustration of this kind of pattern. A simplified analysis of the stages through which we pass in learning to communicate with other people could be as follows:

(*a*) The use of expressive sounds which are not words.
(*b*) The use of single words to convey more complicated ideas
 – as when a toddler says 'Out!' to signify that something ought to be thrown away, or that he wants taking for a walk, or that he has just been for a walk, according to the context.
(*c*) The use of simple sentences.
(*d*) The use of complex sentences.

Now the average adult has gone through all of these stages, but nevertheless uses, at different times, all four methods of communication. He says 'Ouch!' to mean that something hurts, or a sigh to indicate satisfaction; he uses single words, like 'Out!' or 'Quick!' to convey more complex ideas; and he uses both simple and complex sentences.

The reader will see at once that the question of whether moral thinking conforms to the first or the second pattern is one of the greatest importance. If the former is the more appropriate model, we will expect the child, at a given stage in his development to be characterised by a single type of moral judgement, whereas in the latter case we would expect to see a variety of patterns, including some which are typical of more primitive developmental levels.

3. *Parallel phases*

Naturally, development takes place in many directions at once. It may sometimes happen that the signs of two separate lines of development appear to form a single sequence, so that we fail to observe that two different things are going on at once. It is as if we were to observe the various activities which go with a child's learning to walk and talk and to report them as a single sequence of phases. He makes, we might say, simple sounds; then he sits up; says words; stands up; says two-word sentences; crawls, and so on. Of course, no one would really make such a mistake when dealing with two activities which are so obviously different from each other, but when dealing with a subject where the distinction is less obvious it becomes possible to overlook the existence of parallel sequences of phases. Many textbooks report the existence of a sequence of phases to do with learning to walk. It is equally possible to regard these as two parallel sequences to do with acquiring upright stance and the power of locomotion. This is the sort of possibility we must keep in mind when discussing moral development, and a model of this kind will, in fact, be described in the next chapter.

4. *False sequences*

Appearances may mislead completely. We may have what appears to be a straightforward sequence of phases on the first pattern that we discussed, which turns out on investigation to be a by-product of maturation. Again, an example from a different area may help. The stages of a bird learning to fly look like an ordinary sequence of stages in a learning task, but in fact if a bird is confined in such a way that it has no opportunity to go through the earlier stages, it can nevertheless fly when released. The stage it has reached is governed by its level of physical maturity, rather than by the sequence of activities it has carried out. The same sort of thing has been shown to happen in human development, with particular reference to physical activities, like climbing stairs. Maturation plays a much clearer part in physical development than in the development of thinking, but we cannot afford to exclude it as a possibility.

There are therefore two questions to be asked about the development of moral thinking: we want to know not only what are the phases through which a child passes, the concepts and operations of which he is capable at any given point, but also how these phases relate to each other, or which of the above patterns they conform to.

PIAGET: STAGES IN INTELLECTUAL DEVELOPMENT

The psychologist who has been most influential in the study of children's thinking and concept formation is Jean Piaget. Although he has been working in this field for over forty years, it is only comparatively recently that his work has directly influenced our approach in this country, and his methods differ in a number of ways from the approaches which have been developed by psychologists in the English-speaking world. He is not concerned with experimental method in the strict sense of the term, nor has he employed the sophisticated methods of sampling and statistical analysis which have become common in other countries. In some ways, his approach resembles that of a clinician, since his work involves careful and detailed analysis of data concerning a small number of children, and in other respects it resembles, in its careful observation, the approach of a good field naturalist. In its conceptual analysis of the material furnished by the children, it has a great deal in common with the work of the logician.

The experiments are usually deceptively simple. A child is shown a quantity of water in a tall thin jug and, while he is watching, the water is poured into a short wider jug. The experimenter asks whether there is now more water than before, or less. The child's answer gives information about his concepts to do with the conservation of matter. A little girl is asked, 'Have you got a sister?' The answer is yes, she has a sister called Mary. The experimenter asks whether Mary has a sister, and the little girl answers 'No'. We have learnt something very interesting about the child's perception of relationships. In such work, the experimenter is not following a rigidly defined scheme of questions; he is rather exploring the nature of the child's responses to the material and the thought processes that lie behind them.

Piaget and his collaborators in Geneva have built up an extensive theory of the way a child's thought processes develop (17, 18, 19). This theory emphasises two aspects of the child's thinking, which may at first sight appear to be paradoxical. Firstly, the growth of the child's reasoning represents a continuous process. Secondly, the earlier phases of the child's thinking are different in kind, and not merely in degree, from the thought processes of the adult. The child does not merely do the same kind of operation as an adult, but with less efficiency: the operations themselves are different in type.

The theory involves the idea of a number of consecutive phases. A simplified version of these is given below.

1. *Sensori-motor stage* (about 0 to 2 years)

The child is learning to deal with his own perceptual and motor functions, and to fit these together, so that, for example, when he sees a biscuit, he firstly knows that it is an object in the external world, and secondly can co-ordinate his vision and the movements of his hand and arm so as to pick up the biscuit and place it accurately into his mouth. Activities of this kind, though often apparently random, are the basic explorations of the nature of the self and the outside world, the raw material from which the more sophisticated concepts of later life are built up.

2. *Pre-operational or representational stage* (about 2 to 6 years)

The child learns to represent the world by means of symbols – especially linguistic symbols; but he has no real concepts yet, and no true understanding of such matters as causal relationships, which he tends to represent in an animistic way. The rain falls because the clouds are crying. It gets dark because the sun goes to bed. He is not well able to separate goals and means.

3. *Stage of concrete operations* (about 7 to 11 years)

The child begins to use genuine concepts and to apply these to situations and problems, but only insofar as these relate to the world as it can be immediately perceived. There is little generalisation or abstraction.

4. *Stage of formal operations* (from about 12 years)

True generalisation, abstract thinking and hypothetical reasoning become possible for the first time.

It will be seen that we are dealing here with a sequence of phases, such as was discussed at the beginning of this chapter. But which type? It is not always clear which is the model favoured by the authors of the scheme. It is usually regarded as being a simple uni-directional and irreversible sequence of the first type we discussed, but more recently it has seemed that it has been regarded as a cumulative sequence.

This general theory of intellectual development has been quite widely applied to practical questions to do with children's intellectual growth and their learning of school subjects. A number of implications have emerged from this which, as we will see, have clear implications concerning the relevance of developmental schemes to whatever practical measures we take to further the child's moral development. If it is necessary for a child to go through such a sequence in a fixed order, then, even though the highest stage may be our ultimate objective, we must ignore this until the child has reached the penultimate stage. What we can hope to do is to consolidate his experience at his own level, and perhaps by giving him suitable experiences, accelerate his movement to the next one. Suppose that our objective is to enable a child to handle abstract and generalised concepts, and to be able to carry out fully reversible operations with them. If the child is about five years old and working at the pre-operational level, it will be a waste of time to try and teach him directly to carry out formal operations. We must instead concentrate on getting him to the next stage – that of concrete operations. The point is not that the process cannot be accelerated. On the contrary, it can be accelerated a great deal, but this can only be done by concentrating on the next step ahead.

All this has taken us away from direct discussion of moral thinking, but it is a necessary preliminary exercise.

Piaget's work on moral thinking dealt with two separate topics: the child's understanding of rules, and the child's mode of moral thought.

UNDERSTANDING OF RULES

To explore this topic, Piaget used a method of investigation as simple as that used in his enquiry into other topics. The only equipment required was a few marbles. The experimenter gave these to the child and asked to be taught how to play, feigning ignorance so that the child was obliged to formulate and express the rules. It may be thought that there is little connection between a game of marbles and moral behaviour. The technique does however provide a useful device for understanding how children handle rules. As Piaget pointed out, the game has an extremely complex system of rules ... 'a jurisprudence' of its own. The approach also has the advantage that the experimenters are able to compare what the child says about the way the rules work with what he actually does when it comes to applying them to a game.

The subjects in the original enquiry were about twenty children, aged between four and thirteen years. This has sometimes been the subject of criticism. The total number of subjects (which was never stated exactly) is rather small as the basis of a general theory, and they were probably drawn from a very limited social group. However, the jibe that the work merely represents a study of the rules of the game of marbles as played by Swiss middle-class children seems to be unjustified, since the experiments have been repeated with approximately similar results in a number of countries, one of the most recent occasions being on British television.

Analysis of the behaviour of the children in the experiment led to the formulation of a sequence of four stages in the development of a child's use and understanding of rules. In some ways these phases recall the same author's general stages of intellectual development, described above. The stages are:

1. *The motor stage*

This corresponds to the sensori-motor stage in general development, and occupies the same time span. The marbles are handled largely at the dictates of the small child's transient desires or motor habits. His play is not, however, entirely random; he develops a number of fixed patterns of behaviour, but these could probably not be correctly described as rules. Certainly, since the child has not yet begun to co-operate with other children, they cannot be rules in any collective or social sense, even though they do modify or restrain his behaviour.

2. *The egocentric stage*

Between the ages of two and five, the child begins to imitate rules which he sees in the behaviour of other children, but he does not as yet try to co-operate in any real sense. When a number of children at this stage are playing together, they do not make any attempt to arrive at a unified set of rules. In spite of their being together in a physical sense, and in spite of the imitation, each child is playing separately.

3. *Stage of incipient co-operation*

This overlaps with the second stage. The children are now playing together in a real sense. They are trying to win, and therefore they must begin to pay attention to the question of a code of unified rules. But their ideas of rules in general are still vague. They can usually manage to work something out in an actual game, but when the children who take part are questioned separately, they may give contradictory accounts of the rules they have been following.

4. *Stage of codification*

Somewhere about eleven or twelve years, children begin to fix the rules in detail, so that they attain the form which Piaget refers to as jurisprudence. The code of rules is known to and accepted by the general society of children.

This scheme is an account of how the children handled the rules, or followed them, at various ages. But there is another aspect of the child's understanding of rules, which is more important, namely the child's insight into what rules are. In the second part of the investigation, this was dealt with by a number of questions, which, like so many of Piaget's enquiries, were at once deceptively simple and ingenious. The child was asked, for instance, to make up a new rule of his own. When he had done this, he was asked such questions as: 'Would it be all right to play like that with other children?'; 'Is that a "fair" rule?'; 'Is it a real rule?'; 'Could your rule become the way everybody plays?'; 'Do you think your father used these rules when he was a little boy?'.

The answers to such questions suggested another sequence of phases. Since we are not now dealing with the same aspect of the understanding of rules as that which was the subject of the developmental scheme described above, we must be prepared to find that the new sequence does not exactly coincide with the earlier one. This, of course, does not imply that there is any conflict between them. In this scheme, three phases were distinguished:

1. The first stage coincides roughly with the motor stage and the first part of the egocentric stage in the above scheme. At first, of course, the infant has no conception of rules. When,

towards the end of this stage, they begin to influence his play, they are seen as interesting examples rather than as obligations. They have no binding power or force.

2. The second or *transcendental* stage begins towards the end of the egocentric stage and lasts until somewhere about the middle of the stage of incipient co-operation. The child is keenly aware of rules, which are, however, regarded as 'sacred and untouchable, emanating from adults and lasting for ever; every suggested alteration strikes the child as a transgression'.

3. At the third stage, the rule is regarded as an arrangement arising from *mutual consent*. It now becomes possible to alter rules, provided that the other players in the game agree. Piaget regards this final stage, being based on mutual respect and co-operation and on consideration of the rights of others, as the one which represents the achievement of the true understanding of the nature of rules, and the one which is most relevant to genuine moral development.

MODE OF MORAL THOUGHT – TWO MORALITIES OF CHILDHOOD

We see, then, in the development of the child's understanding of rules, two major shifts of orientation. Of these, the second, that between the transcendental and the final stages, is regarded as being the most interesting and the most important. This is because it represents a change of both thinking and attitude which keeps reappearing in other parts of the survey, and which has a bearing on other aspects of the child's moral judgement.

Piaget goes on to explore the child's ideas about justice and fairness, about punishment, and about such concepts as telling lies. The method is mainly to tell children stories and ask them questions about the situations described. The following pair of stories illustrate how this works.

1. There was once a little girl called Marie. She wanted to give her mother a nice surprise, and to cut out a piece of sewing for her, but she did not know how to use the scissors properly, and cut a big hole in her dress.

2. A little girl called Margaret went and took her mother's

scissors one day when her mother was out. She played with them for a bit, then, as she didn't know how to use them properly, she made a little hole in her dress.

The reader will see that the pair of stories involves a balancing by the person questioned of the relative importance of motive as against the extent of damage. Again, there was no formal schedule of questions. The children simply listened to the stories, and told the investigator which of the two children was naughtier, or which should be punished more severely, or what was the fairest course of action. The child's replies were followed by a free exploration of the thought processes which seemed to be involved, just as was done in the enquiries about rules.

The concept of lying was investigated by question and answer, such questions being put to the child as 'Is it worse to tell a lie to an adult than to another child?' or 'Are lies which are so big that no one would believe them better than smaller lies, which might be believed?'.

A number of connected findings emerged from this part of the enquiry, all of which are a reflection of this difference between the transcendental and co-operative stages of the understanding of rules. Children at the transcendental rule stage tend to stress, for instance, actual damage without regard to motive. In the pair of stories quoted above, the younger children say that the girl who made the big hole was more to blame, in spite of the fact that she was trying to be helpful. 'The one who wanted to help her mother a little is the naughtiest, because she made a big hole; she got scolded.' In another story, the boy who smashed a dozen cups which were on a tray behind the door was more to blame (although he could not have known the cups were there) than the child who broke a single cup while climbing on the larder shelves in order to steal some jam.

The shift from transcendental rules to mutual consent type of rules, then, corresponds to a parallel tendency to move from the principle of objective responsibility to subjective responsibility. That is, to move from judgements which simply take account of the nature of the consequences to those which take into account intention and motive. The shift is not, in practice, as clear-cut as it might appear in a description of this kind. There is considerable overlap, and some specificity, in that it was found to be quite possible for the same child to express the two types of judgement with regard to different situations.

Children's judgements of telling lies showed a similar developmental pattern. At the transcendental stage, a lie told to an adult is more reprehensible than one told to a small child. The seriousness of a lie is in direct proportion to its 'size', no matter how great the resulting improbability. It is not until the stage of co-operation that we see the more sophisticated argument that more plausible lies are worse.

So, too, with the child's idea of fairness. At the transcendental stage, the child thinks of fairness as being an absolute – even an arithmetic – principle. It is not until later that the idea of individual needs begins to moderate it.

Each area of the investigation presented an overall picture which was similar to the second and third phases of the child's understanding of rules. Transcendental rules give way to co-operative ones; objective to subjective responsibility; arithmetic ideas of fairness to those which take account of individual needs; retributive punishment to punishment which takes account of motive. Piaget draws together the findings in these separate areas by suggesting that they are specific instances of two overriding stages of moral thinking, stages which are in such marked contrast to each other that he describes them as 'two moralities'.

Heteronomous morality

This is an authoritarian moral code, imposed on the child by the adult world. It is non-rational in character, and it is characterised by moral realism. That is to say, the rules have a permanent and objective value apart from the individuals who obey them. Its further characteristics have already been described, for they are the first modes of response in each of the examples given above to illustrate the appearance of this attitude shift.

Autonomous morality

This is an egalitarian and democratic morality, based on mutual respect and co-operation. It is rational and it arises from the interaction between the child and his peers. *Piaget sees nothing in the first morality which can give rise to the second.* The child's sense of justice is, in fact, reckoned to be largely independent of adult influences, and it 'requires nothing more for its development than the mutual respect and solidarity which holds amongst children themselves. It is often at the expense of the adult, and not because of him, that the notions of just and unjust find their way into the youthful mind'.

This view of the development of moral thinking has been very influential. Before moving on to examine more recent approaches, three points are worth making.

Firstly, the use of the two opposed terms, heteronomous and autonomous, may be a little misleading. 'Heteronomous' means 'subject to the guidance or rule of another'. That is, in this case, moral rules and guidance originate *outside* the individual; they are imposed on him from the environment. 'Autonomous' gives us to understand that rules are not so imposed; that the individual's moral standards are independent of such imposition.

It is possible that part of the changed attitude observed by Piaget is due to the increasing influence in the middle years of childhood of the peer group, something which has been so widely reported that it has become a commonplace of developmental psychology. If this is so, then, although we may trace some elements of genuine autonomy in the aspects of behaviour grouped together under that heading, at least part of the change results from a substitution of the heteronomy of the peer group for the heteronomy of the adult world.

Secondly, it would be a mistake to regard this theory of the two moralities of childhood – no matter how useful we may find the distinction – as providing a complete picture: it makes no mention of the role of conscience. As we have seen, conscience is seen by many workers as a phenomenon which succeeds heteronomy; it may, in fact, be regarded as an internalisation or introjection of heteronomous morality. A complete picture of the child's moral behaviour should include this type of moral judgement.

Both of the above points have been taken up by later workers, whose conclusions will be described presently.

Thirdly, although the four stages in the child's use of rules seem to form the kind of phase sequence which we associate with Piaget's other work, the two moralities do not. As we have seen, Piaget, rather than regarding heteronomous morality as being a necessary precursor of autonomy, explicitly states that he sees nothing in the first which can give rise to the second. This statement is perhaps rather surprising, since it appears to owe more to the then prevailing climate of educational opinion than to the principles expounded elsewhere in Piaget's work, with its stress on continuity of development in spite of qualitative differences. Although Piaget's work in this field has been extremely influential, we shall see that later psychologists have not followed him in this matter of discontinuity, taking rather as their model the type of phase pattern which is more typical of the Piagetian approach. Even so, the idea of movement from heteronomy to autonomy is one which is not only extremely useful, but which has survived up to the present time.

PECK AND HAVIGHURST: A MORAL TYPOLOGY

A more recent attempt at providing a sequence of phases which represents moral thinking is Peck and Havighurst's work on the psychology of character development (20). Although the work is wider in its intention than a simple analysis of concept formation, it will be seen that it is essentially concerned with different orientations to moral problems, and so resembles moral thinking more closely than it does the other headings in this book.

Peck and Havighurst studied a small community in the American Middle West. Initially, they administered various tests – moral ideology, emotional response and other measures – on all the 120 children who were born in 1933, and who were living in the community in 1943. They also obtained character ratings by teachers and by peers at various points as the sample grew up. The work is based, however, more specifically on a much smaller cross-section of this population, consisting of thirty-four children, an equal number of boys and girls. These children were studied by a variety of techniques – projective personality tests, sentence completion tests, interviews, and observations carried out by fieldworkers who lived in the town and got to know the children well. The material thus gathered was submitted to a number of analyses of a high degree of sophistication and complexity.

Research workers in such a complex field as this are inevitably faced with a dilemma when it comes to designing a piece of research. It should be remembered that Peck and Havighurst's approach represents a solution to this problem which lies at one extreme of the continuum of possible answers: they settled for high-powered analysis of a complex mass of data about a very small number of subjects. It should also be remembered that not all psychologists are entirely satisfied about the reliability and usefulness of some of the measures – notably the projective personality tests – used in this work. Nevertheless, the importance of the findings should not be underestimated, and, as we shall see, the research gives a more detailed postulated theory of moral development than we have so far seen.

Peck and Havighurst postulate five moral character types, which are conceived as successive stages in the individual's development.

1. *Amoral, in infancy*

In an earlier chapter, we discussed the psychopathic personality. Much of what was said at that time applies to this character type. The amoral person sees other people as means to self-gratification and is completely egocentric. He lacks moral principles and conscience in both the senses we have proposed for the word. The picture is in many ways that of an infant whose socialisation has hardly begun.

2. *Expedient, in early childhood*

The expedient person tends to act in accordance with the mores of his society, but only in order to avoid punishment, or in order to gain an advantage. He is not concerned about other people's welfare, except insofar as such concern is to his own advantage.

Peck and Havighurst regard this type, too, as being basically egocentric. His 'morality' is in a sense precarious, since if his only reason for keeping the rules is to secure his own advantage, he is quite prepared to abandon the rules when it is no longer in his own interests to conform to them. This pattern of behaviour is said by the authors to be characteristic of younger children, who have learnt to have a regard for the power of adults to give rewards or administer punishments, and who moderate their behaviour on that account whenever a grown-up is around. When they are on their own, however, they quickly relapse into the egocentricity which is more natural to them.

3(a). Conforming, in later childhood

The conformist is one whose guiding principle is 'what is done'. This may appear in a number of forms – sticking to the rules of the group, honouring the tradition of one's society. Unlike the two earlier patterns of thought, it does lead to a stable orientation towards questions of right and wrong, but this is not something that arises from a generalised moral principle – unless you count as a principle conforming to what others do. The conformist tends to approach each situation separately, applying to it the appropriate rule or convention, and for this reason we may expect to find some degree of specificity in his behaviour.

3(b). Irrational conscientious, in later childhood

This person judges situations according to his own internal standards of right and wrong, paying little attention to whether or not his decision is approved by the people around him. 'Non-rational' would perhaps have been a clearer term than 'irrational'. We have already discussed the implications of the word. Such principles are applied in a somewhat rigid manner; an act is good or bad because the individual intuitively feels it to be so, and not because of its effects on others.

This type, too, results in stability of moral behaviour, even though this is a rigid stability. The reader will recognise that much of the discussion in the earlier chapter on conscience is relevant here.

4. Rational altruistic, in later childhood

This is the highest level of moral maturity in the Peck and Havighurst scheme. Those who function on this basis not only have a stable set of moral principles, but apply them flexibly and objectively in terms of whether the consequences of a given act are good or harmful. As the name suggests, these consequences relate mainly to other people. This word should not give a false impression. We should, for instance, distinguish between self-sacrifice to a useful end, and neurotic self-sacrifice which has no function other than an obscure self-satisfaction. The rational altruistic person is aware of the norms of his society and of the promptings of his own conscience, but he is able to observe the spirit of the rules rather than remain confined to a rigid adherence to their letter because of his regard for consequences.

The reader will have noticed that this is not a straightforward developmental sequence. The third stage is subdivided and the descriptions of the conforming and irrational conscientious types will doubtless recall the earlier discussion, in chapter 4, on inner- and other-directed people, and the distinction between guilt and shame. You will remember that these were seen as opposed character types. Peck and Havighurst were aware of this work and suggested that these phases may represent parallel or alternative stages on the way to rational altruism, so that the scheme of moral development may be represented as shown below.

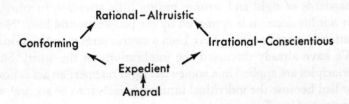

You will have noticed that this developmental scheme serves two functions. It is at once a sequence of developmental stages and a moral typology. That is, it serves not only to tell us how far an individual's moral thinking has progressed, but also to *classify* individuals into the 'expedient type', the 'conforming type', and so on. This kind of classification is very attractive, since it provides a quick and convenient way of summing up the moral behaviour of people with whom we come into contact, but its very ease may present a danger in that it can lead us to make too facile judgements, slotting people into pigeon-holes. The diffi-culties arising from such a process were discussed in chapter 2.

A moral typology can never be more than a rough guide to the individual's *predominant* response. We would not expect to see, in real life, many 'pure' types, such as those described above – that is, people who are motivated on every occasion by considerations of expediency, conscience, or altruism. More typical is the tendency for an individual's behaviour to be characterised by more than one of these patterns. (In fairness, it should be pointed out that this warning is intended to deal with a possible mis-understanding on the part of the reader, rather than to ascribe a misleading interpretation to the authors of the typology, who do make a point of drawing attention to the dangers of thinking in terms of 'pure' types.)

Of course, there are exceptions. The psychopath, for instance, seems to be fixated at the most primitive level of moral thought, but this is entirely consistent with the developmental aspect of the scheme if we assume that the pattern is a cumulative one (and, of course, at stage three, parallel). What this means in practice is that we are talking about the individual's *capacity* for certain types of moral thought. Progress up the developmental ladder implies an increase in the individual's total repertoire. Since the psycho-path has not moved on from the earliest stage, he has only one type of moral thinking available. The person who has reached the rational altruistic level, on the other hand, has five. It also follows from this view of Peck and Havighurst's work that the individual's moral type, or typical form of moral thinking, is by no means necessarily the same thing as the highest level he has attained.

We should be clear, too, that to postulate a developmental pattern of this sort does not mean that we expect everybody to reach the highest stage. Indeed, even if it were true that only a minority of people reached this point, it would still deserve its place at the top rung of the ladder if the only way to get there were by the lower rungs. In this case, Peck and Havighurst pointed out that the majority of the adolescents in their survey did not, in fact, reach the rational altruistic level.

F

KOHLBERG: GROWTH TOWARDS AUTONOMY

A more recent, and very important study of moral development is that carried out by Lawrence Kohlberg (21). This work follows more directly in the tradition of Piaget, but is concerned with rather larger samples (Kohlberg's original study was based on seventy-two boys, aged 10, 13 and 16), a standardised interviewing procedure, and a method of interpreting the results which pays some attention to such difficulties as whether the method of interpretation is biased by the judge who is carrying it out.

Kohlberg's method is essentially to explore the child's moral judgements by means of the moral dilemma. A number of such dilemmas are put to the child in the form of stories: a man's wife is dying. There is a drug which might save her, but the husband cannot raise the amount of money asked by the only supplier, a profiteering chemist. Is he justified in stealing some of the drug? If he is arrested, what action should the judge take? Again, a fireman is faced with the dilemma of doing his duty and rescuing some people trapped by a disastrous fire, or going off to see to his own family, who are in equal danger. What should he do? Why?

These stories were cast in the form of a lengthy interview (each one lasting about two hours), in which attention was given not only to the child's solution but also to the reasons underlying this solution. The examination of the interview records dealt with a wide variety of questions, such as the child's concept of rights and justice, his views on the importance of intentions as opposed to consequences, and so on.

Although this work covered many different aspects of morality, it will be seen that the dilemmas incorporated in the stories tended to be of a particular kind, namely conflict between obedience to legal and social rules, or the commands of authority and human needs, or the welfare of other people.

In spite of the complexity of the analysis of this work, and the many different aspects of moral thinking which were distinguished, Kohlberg's conclusions were that moral judgements are characterised by an overall developmental pattern, which consists of six stages, these being grouped into three levels:

1. *Pre-moral level*
   Stage I: Punishment and obedience orientation. Rules are obeyed to avoid punishment.
   Stage II: Naïve instrumental hedonism. The child conforms in order to obtain rewards.

2. *Morality of conventional role conformity*
   Stage III: 'Good boy morality' of maintaining good relations. The child conforms to avoid disapproval.
   Stage IV: Authority maintaining morality. The child conforms to avoid censure by authorities and resulting guilt.

3. *Morality of self-accepted moral principles*
   Stage V: Morality of contract. A duty is defined in terms of contract, general avoidance of violation of the rights of others.
   Stage VI: Morality of individual principles of conscience. The child conforms to avoid self-condemnation.

Kohlberg makes it clear that he regards this developmental pattern as being a simple series of consecutive phases, such as we described in the early part of the chapter. Progress through them is uni-directional and irreversible.

INTER-RELATION OF ALL ASPECTS
It would be easy to overemphasise the points of difference between these approaches and others like them. It is true that their terminology is different, and that they are not in perfect agreement as regards the relative positions in time of some of the stages of development. Nevertheless, it is possible to construct a detailed concordance of different schemes of this sort, with cross-references between the names of the various types of moral thinking. (Such a combined scheme can be found in Kay (22).)

For our purposes, it is probably sufficient to point out that all these schemes have in common the idea of a fairly small number of phases, which are seen as either consecutive or cumulative. In spite of the obvious disagreements, the direction of growth is the same in each case. An egocentric amoral early phase is replaced by some form of heteronomy, which in turn gives way to autonomy. All the work reviewed here, then, points to moral development as being a movement towards moral autonomy, a view which is in agreement with the assessment of the types of moral thinking as it would be made by most moral philosophers.

We began the chapter by referring to moral thinking, but our discussion of the topic has led us to consider a much wider area. The ideas of conscience and conformism have proved relevant. So, too, has the idea of concern – without it genuine altruism, which tends to figure as the final phase, cannot exist. This is, of course, an example of what was said at the beginning of the book about the impossibility of compartmentalising moral development. All the aspects of the subject are inter-related. It is possible, for some purposes, to classify explanations of moral development. We may say that some are concerned with how sanctions change, others with changing patterns of motivation, others with changing attitudes. Although such distinctions are helpful in some contexts, it is probably more useful to stress the inter-relatedness of these various facets. A given attitude sensitises its possessor to certain sanctions, and insofar as it influences behaviour, it may be regarded as a motive. Peck and Havighurst's scheme is usually described as being concerned with motivation – indeed the authors themselves describe it in this way, but expediency does not only imply a different motive from rational altruism – the implied attitude to other people is different, too. The conforming and the conscientious persons differ from each other, not only in motive and attitude, but also in the sanctions to which they respond.

These models of moral development have then a great deal in common, not least in their implications for moral education. They argue that autonomy and altruism are not only the most desirable ends, but are also chronologically the latest phenomena to arrive on the scene. The use of a pattern of sequential phases suggests that even though rational altruism and autonomy may be our ultimate goals, they cannot be made the subject of explicit teaching until the child has reached a certain stage in development. The child cannot get to the final stage until the penultimate one has been attained, no matter how hard the educator may try, and the aim must therefore be to accelerate growth through all the stages. This brings us to the perhaps paradoxical position that, in order to teach a child to be autonomous, we must first teach him to be dependent for his moral judgements on others.

But not everyone would agree that a sequential model is the most appropriate. It is true that evidence carefully gathered cannot be lightly set aside, but we can say that the sequential approach is perhaps a surprising one when we compare it with our everyday experience. Is it true that when a person attains a stage of making autonomous judgements based on his predictions of the consequences of his actions on other people, he necessarily stops having irrational or intuitive feelings of what is right and wrong, equally irrational sensations of guilt, or even an awareness of the probability of reward and punishment? Our interpretations of everyday experience can be very misleading, of course. But in this case we have, too, the observations of psychoanalysts and clinical psychologists that our rational conscious behaviour co-exists with a stream of less rational components of personality, which are both moral and amoral, and which survive from more primitive stages of development. Of the studies so far discussed, only that of Peck and Havighurst takes significant account of this area of study and its findings.

If, of course, we come upon evidence that moral development is not a uni-directional process, then this will change our whole orientation to moral education. It is clear that a solution to this problem is of the greatest importance.

SUMMARY

A number of developmental schemes were considered. Although they differ in detail, they are all characterised by seeing moral development as a series of consecutive phases proceeding from the heteronomous and expedient to the autonomous and altruistic.

FURTHER READING

See Piaget (17), Brearley (18), Piaget & Isaacs (19), Peck (20), Kohlberg (21), and Kay (22).

6 Modes of Moral Thought

Four mothers:

> You mustn't pull your little sister's hair like that!
> – Why not?
> Because I say so!

> You mustn't pull your little sister's hair like that!
> – Why not?
> Because you mustn't!

> You mustn't pull your little sister's hair like that!
> – Why not?
> Because I'll smack you if you do!

> You mustn't pull your little sister's hair like that!
> – Why not?
> Because it hurts her and makes her cry.

At the end of the last chapter, we discussed the possibility of an alternative approach to the question of moral thinking and development. Such an approach is suggested by some of the results of a survey of children's moral thinking (mentioned in an earlier chapter), which was sponsored by the Farmington Trust. This survey was concerned with the moral thinking of children and young people between the ages of four and eighteen.

The rationale of the research is simple, namely that differences in moral thinking may be inferred from the various justifications offered by different people for a similar moral judgement. In this respect it resembles some aspects of the studies discussed in the last chapter. Thus, to give an example not included in the research itself, if you were to ask a number of people why it is wrong to approach a busy pedestrian-crossing at eighty miles-an-hour, you might be offered a number of different reasons:

'You can lose your licence for that sort of thing.'
'It's against the law.'
'You might kill somebody.'

It seems fair to assume that these different reasons imply different ways of thinking about the problem. Mindful of a point made in the previous chapter, we may perhaps go further, and infer corresponding differences in attitude and motive.

In the research, children were asked, in a standardised interview, about a number of simple moral concepts: good, bad, ought, being fair, lying, stealing and bullying. In each section of the interview, the child was asked to explain what he understood by the concept and then to say whether it was right or wrong – i.e. to make a moral judgement about it. For instance:

'What does "bullying" mean?'
'Can you tell me about somebody doing that?'
'Is it right, or wrong, to bully?'

As you would expect from the nature of the particular concepts chosen, nearly all the children spoken to were in agreement about the moral judgement they gave. The children were then asked why it was right (or wrong); how they could tell it was right, who told them, and so on. Stories were not used, and any material offered to the child by the interviewer was avoided on the grounds that it might indicate a particular kind of reply. For the very young children, instead of relying on verbal concepts, the interviewer had a glove puppet which acted the ideas where this was possible.

This led to the design of a simple and flexible research instrument which could be used with a wide variety of ages. The question: 'Why is it wrong to steal?' may be a very simple one, or a very complex one, depending on the person to whom it is addressed. The simplicity of the interview also meant that a considerably larger sample could be used than in the surveys discussed above. (This is the diametrically opposite solution of the problems of research design to that favoured by Peck and

Havighurst.) 790 children were interviewed altogether, from a wide variety of areas in England.

The size of the sample meant also that representatives of each year group could be included, rather than having to rely on a few year groups.

The first task was to decide on the categories to be used in interpreting the data. Clearly, this is a crucial matter, since the choice of scoring categories can, in some circumstances, determine the results of the work. 200 consecutively-gathered interview records were examined, with the object of distinguishing as many mutually exclusive categories of response as possible. This led to the description of seventeen different types of answer. These are listed below, with a few examples of each taken from actual interview records.

1. *Amoral, uncontrolled responses*

These are similar to Peck and Havighurst's first stage. They reflect an approach to right and wrong which is amoral and impulse-governed, and generally express the idea that you should do what you want to do.

> 'There's nothing wrong with telling lies . . . you just do it if it suits you.'
> – Can you think of a time when it's all right to steal?
> 'Yes if it's something you really want.'
> – When is it all right to bully?
> 'If you really hate the person.'

2. *Authoritarian responses*

These are concerned with *personal* authority. The command or wish or statement of some individual is quoted as sufficient justification for the moral judgement.

> – Why is it wrong to tell lies?
> 'Teacher says so.'
> – Why is it wrong to hit people?
> 'Daddy says I mustn't.'

There are some signs in the interview records of a line of development which leads to changes in the authority figure quoted at different ages. It appears to change from a parent or teacher through more distant figures like the clergyman, the magistrates, to distant figures like the Pope or the Prime Minister.

3. *Conforming responses*
Conformity to the norms of a social group is taken as sufficient justification for the moral judgement. We are not here referring so much to explicit formalised rules (see the next category) as response to informal pressures from one's peers.

'All the children in our class say you should own up.'
'We don't do that in our club.'
'Everybody considers that it's wrong.'

4. *Legalist responses*
The child appeals to a generalised and formalised authority as the basis of a moral judgement.

'Stealing is wrong because it's against the law.'
'Smoking is wrong because it's against the school rules.'
'Murder is wrong because there's a law against it.'

5. *Mass communications*
Statements in newspapers, on the radio, or, more frequently, on television, as the basis for a moral judgement.

– Is it wrong to steal?
'Yes.'
– Why is it wrong to steal?
'Well the man says so that comes on the telly.'
– And why is it wrong to smoke?
'I dunno – well, there was a programme about it on the telly.'

In fact, answers of this kind were by no means so frequent as the pessimists would have led us to expect.

6. *Empathic responses*
This is not an entirely satisfactory name, but the possible alternatives, such as altruistic responses, seem to imply too high a level of sophistication. In this category, we include those answers

which are based on a perception of the feelings and needs of other people.

– Why is it wrong to bully people?
'You hurt them and make them cry.'
– Can you tell me an example of a good thing to do?
'Helping an old age pensioner across the road.'
– Why is that good?
'Because they need it – they can't manage too well on their own.'

7. *Theoretical generalisations*

Under this heading come arguments of various kinds, based on theories of what would happen if conduct of the kind in question were general.

'Society gets on better if everybody tells the truth.'
'Civilisation would break down if stealing was OK.'
'If people weren't fair, there'd be wars all the time.'

8. *Utilitarian responses*

A small number of responses from older subjects bears a strong resemblance to the altruistic-utilitarian and rational-utilitarian positions in moral philosophy. These responses are not always clearly formulated from the philosopher's point of view, but since they are characterised by generalised other-relatedness seen as a rule which should govern behaviour, they are grouped together in this category.

– What does wrong mean?
'Just about anything could be wrong if other people's interests are involved. The point is, you ought not to do things which are damaging to others.'

9. *Expedient responses*

In these answers the subject indicates that he believes in his behaviour being modified or controlled, but this is motivated by considerations of his own advantage rather than by anything that could properly be described as a moral principle. He does this, or does not do that, in order to gain a reward or an advantage, or to avoid a punishment.

'I'm good because Mummy gives me more sweets.'
'Bullying is wrong because you get the cane for it.'
'If you're in business, you get on better in the long run if you're fair.'

10. *Guilt avoidance*

The subject modifies his behaviour in order to avoid feelings of guilt afterwards. This may be regarded as a special case of the expedient response, but one which involves some degree of psychological insight as an extra dimension. The discussion in chapter 4 on two aspects of conscience is relevant to this category and the following one, and also to irrational inhibition (q.v.).

'You don't steal because you'd worry about it afterwards.'
'You'd have it on your mind.'
'You keep on remembering it afterwards.'

11. *Social expediency*

The distinction between guilt and shame was discussed in connection with the idea of conscience. We are here dealing with the avoidance of other-directed anxiety as a motive for the control of behaviour. The subject is concerned about 'loss of face'.

'I couldn't face people if they knew I'd been pinching.'
'I wouldn't want the other kids to think of me as a thief.'
'Telling lies is wrong because it gets you a bad reputation.'

Like expediency, this type of response has its positive aspect.

'Helping people is good because they get a good opinion of you.'

12. *Irrational inhibition*

This is an example of Peck and Havighurst's irrational-conscientious category. It appears in the interview records as a clear moral judgement, for which no reason can be supplied – an intuitive moral judgement.

'It's just wrong, I don't know why.'
'I've always known that – my own brains told me.'
– Who told you it was wrong to steal?
'No one told me. It's just commonsense.'

Answers like this may be produced, of course, to some extent by the subject's inability to express himself adequately, but it was clear to the interviewers that such an explanation would not cover all cases. The intuitive judgements were frequently defended with determined and dogged indignation by subjects who were quite well able to provide reasons for other sections of the interview.

13. *Ego-ideal*

Although this term has been borrowed from the Freudian pantheon, it should not be taken to imply in this context a particular view about how it was formed – it is simply a convenient name for a particular class of response in which the subject refers to some ideal version of himself as his standard of comparison.

> 'I'm not the kind of person to do that.'
> 'I'm too big to do that.'
> 'I wouldn't like to think of myself as a sneak.'

The list of categories originally published contained rather more types of response than this. The above, however, as will be seen presently, may be regarded as a self-contained and cohesive scheme. The extra categories were either special cases of those already quoted, or else they did not exclude the possibility of an answer falling into one of the groups already described. The two examples of this latter type are perhaps worth looking at in passing. These are:

Autonomous responses

The subject showed he was aware of a general moral rule covering the topic being discussed, but is willing to make an exception in certain cases as a result of weighing what Kohlberg calls human values.

> 'White lies are all right, because although telling lies is wrong, it might be worse to upset someone when there's no real reason for it.'
> 'Bullying is wrong, but if there's been an accident and someone was too much in a state of shock to help the injured, it might be all right to bully him out of it if his help was really needed.'

A moment's thought will show why this response must be considered separately from the others. It is, of course, a more complex form of answer, involving a relationship between two simple ones. Clearly it cannot be placed in its developmental context until the analysis of the simpler categories is understood.

Religious responses

This is not a classification which relates directly to our present purposes (though that is not to say that religious belief is irrelevant to morality). To classify a child's answer as religious is saying something about the *source* of the judgement rather than about the *type* of thinking. Religious answers may themselves be classified into the categories given above.

'Being good is doing what God wants.'
'. . . following the Ten Commandments.'
'You're good so that you don't go to hell when you die.'
'You should love one another.'

(These additional classifications are not included in what follows below. This is not because we wish to minimise their importance, but because they are a separate topic which requires separate examination.)

One result, then, of using a large number of subjects is that this leads to a greater number of categories of answer, which discriminate more finely. Even if we limit ourselves to those types of answer listed in the main group above, we have thirteen, as opposed to the four, five or six used in earlier classifications. We are bound to ask, however, whether these may not be grouped into some simpler scheme, particularly since (as was pointed out in listing them) some of them appear to resemble each other, even on a superficial examination.

Such a further classification has been worked out and it leads us to a number of conclusions which enable us to relate this work to some of that already described above. In the first place, we can see that all of the responses, except one, imply the existence of some form of control or modification of behaviour, even though the reasons for this may be very different. This suggests that the pre-moral, uncontrolled response should be separated from all of the others, so that we distinguish between the pre-moral, on the one hand, and the moral and para-moral on the other. The remaining twelve categories seem to fall into four groups. These are:

1. Empathic responses, theoretical generalisations, utilitarian responses.
2. Expedient responses, guilt-avoiding responses, shame-avoiding responses.
3. Authoritarian responses, conforming responses, legalist responses, mass communications.
4. Irrational inhibition, ego-ideal.

The presence of four groups of this kind raises the question of whether we can account for them in terms of the interaction of two factors. This seems to be possible. The first factor, which is common to groups 1 and 2, but not 3 and 4, is concerned with whether or not the subject is oriented towards the consequences of an act in making a moral judgement. That is, whether he assesses the consequences – irrespective of whether these affect himself or other people – as opposed to referring the question to some absolute criterion.

We have, then, a dimension of moral thinking, similar to the dimensions referred to in the first chapter, which may be described in the usual way by naming the characteristics of its two poles. We may thus think about this dimension as *consequence* versus *criterion* orientation; or *thinking* versus *referring*; or *considering* versus *obeying*. This dimension may relate closely to what many moral philosophers have in mind when they talk about the rationality of moral behaviour.

A second dimension, which contrasts groups 2 and 4 with 1 and 3, is concerned with whether the subject is oriented towards himself or other people, and may be named quite simply self- or other-relatedness.

SCHEME OF PERSONALITY DESCRIPTION IN A MORAL TYPOLOGY

We have already seen that where dimensions of this sort can be regarded as being orthogonal to each other, we have a more comprehensive scheme of personality description. If we can assume a similar relationship in the present case, we have a scheme of four types of moral thinking preceded by a pre-moral stage, a scheme which, as will be seen below, corresponds very closely to that suggested by Peck and Havighurst, thus providing an independent confirmation of their results, based on an entirely different method.

This scheme is given below. The names of Peck and Havighurst's moral types are shown in brackets.

(a) *Amoral, uncontrolled* (Amoral)

The child's response is impulse-governed, directed to the gratification of his own desires, without regard to either expedient or moral considerations.

(b) *Self-considering* (Expedient)

A situation is evaluated in terms of its consequences, but these consequences relate to the subject himself. They may be matters of naïve expediency – thinking in terms of rewards and punishments – or they may have a more sophisticated element, in which case the subject is thinking of his own emotional or social discomfort.

(c) *Self-obeying* (Irrational-conscientious)

The problem is not evaluated, but is simply referred to an internalised or introjected rule or criterion. In this group, we place the inhibitory aspects of conscience and comparison with an ideal self.

(d) *Other-obeying* (Conforming)

Again, the problem is not evaluated, but is referred to an *external* authority. We distinguish between various types of authority, which range from a personal authority figure to the social or peer group, and to such abstract embodiments of authority as the law.

(e) Other-considering (Rational-altruistic)

The problem is evaluated in terms of its consequences for other people. In this group, we find a number of altruistic and utilitarian forms of moral thinking.*

The relationship between these groups may be seen in the following table.

		CONSIDERING OR (THINKING)	OBEYING OR (REFERRING)
SELF		Expedient	Irrational-inhibition
		Guilt-avoiding	Ego-ideal
		Shame-avoiding	
OTHER		Empathic	Authoritarian
		Theoretical-generalisation	Conforming
		Rational-utilitarian	Legalist
			Mass communications

Although, as we have said, this pattern is in broad agreement with the Peck and Havighurst data, it does differ in that it suggests that we are dealing, not with simple categories, but with very much broader ones, each of which is itself composed of a number of distinguishable types of response. We shall see presently that this is an important point. These broader classifications will be referred to below as 'modes of moral thinking'. The data confirms, too, the Peck and Havighurst view that these are not 'pure' types. An individual's responses are commonly scattered through three or four modes, one of which might be numerically slightly preponderant. Often there are marked differences in the mode of thought preferred for different topics (you will remember that seven such topics were included in the interviews). This will recall the work on specificity discussed in the first chapter.

* More recent, separate, work suggests that there may be factor analytic evidence in support of this scheme – Williams, N. and Sumner, R. (in progress).

STAGES IN DEVELOPMENT

From the point of view of development, however, the question is this: in which order do these modes of thought appear? Or do we look for a model of a different kind?

A final answer to these questions must wait until the detailed statistical analysis of the material has been carried out, but certain facts about the distribution of children's answers are already clear.

1. There is a tendency for children to apply different modes of thought to at least some of the various moral questions raised in the interviews.
2. The older the child, the greater the number of different kinds of response obtained. Since the number of questions is the same in all cases, this must imply greater overlap with increasing age.
3. Even at the earliest age groups interviewed, responses belonging to each of the four modes are already present. This is a most important observation. It means that it is at least unlikely that the four modes are in the form of a developmental sequence, and that it is certain that, even if such a sequence were present, the timing would be quite different from that suggested by earlier studies. Four-year-old children are quite capable, it seems, of even the most 'advanced' forms of moral thought. Of course, at this age, they exist in a simple form. (As you will remember, it is the altruistic response which is generally regarded as chronologically more advanced.)

> – Why is it wrong to steal?
> "Cos they might be looking for it.'
> – Why is it wrong to bully people?
> "Cos it makes them cry.'

As the child gets older, other considering answers reflect the various changes which are taking place in his capacities. His intelligence, his power of forming concepts, and of carrying out operations with them, develop, and this leads to the appearance of more sophisticated forms of response within this mode of

G

thinking, such as those which we have described as arising from theoretical generalisations or altruistic and utilitarian considerations. Piaget's work on the development of the child's thinking, referred to in the previous chapter, is obviously relevant to this.

The same pattern of increasing sophistication and maturity may be observed in two of the other modes of moral thinking.

Other-obeying

The earliest forms of other-obeying response seem to be those which are concerned with simple personal authority – 'because Daddy says so'; 'Sir says it's wrong'. As we have seen in other accounts of moral development, these give place to conformity to social norms, while that authoritarian response which is founded on a respect for the law represents a degree of abstraction which is not possible until much later.

Self-considering

The most primitive form in which this mode of thinking appears is that which involves naïve reward and punishment expediency. As the child grows older, his capacity for visualising pleasant or unpleasant consequences is improved, so that we see the emergence of psychological and social expediency responses.

Self-obeying

This mode of thought may be the exception in that it may be more static than the others. Certainly, our review of the literature on conscience does not give any lead as to what 'development' would mean in this area.

The suggestion is, then, that we are dealing here with parallel developmental sequences, which reflect the child's increasing maturity in general, rather than any specifically moral development. These separate sequences are echoed in some of the versions of moral development already described. While the four main modes which remain constant recall the Peck and Havighurst material, the consecutive phases described above can be made to fit quite closely with Kohlberg's scheme, or Piaget's work.

But this is not the only kind of growth. You will remember

that older children tended to give a greater number of answers of different kinds as justifications for a single moral judgement. We can account for this in terms of a *generalisation effect*. Now we had better make sure what we mean by the word 'generalisation' in this context. It does not refer to the abstract formulation of generalisations, or the creating of abstract generalised rules. Indeed, it is a process which can take place in the absence of any advanced thought processes at all. For our present purpose, 'generalisation' refers to the tendency for a response to become attached to wider, or more general, situations than those which originally gave rise to it. We have already discussed a process which illustrates this, when thinking about the growth of concern for other people. The young child has concern for a very small number of people with whom he comes in contact. This concern becomes transferred to wider and wider circles, until, in some cases at any rate, it is so generalised as to include starving children in other parts of the world, earthquake victims whom one has never met, and so on. Confusion can arise because such a process is frequently accompanied by the capacity to form abstract and general concepts of the kind which we refer to in everyday speech as generalisations. But it must be clear that there are at least some cases where you find the attitude without the consciously formulated general statement, or where the concept is formulated (perhaps insincerely) without the generalised attitude.

Perhaps another example would help. It is possible to teach a puppy to respond to the command 'Outside!' by going into the garden. If the command is given when the puppy is in a strange house, it may become confused. This is because the response related in the first instance to a very specific situation, namely going from its own house to its own garden. Eventually, of course, it will respond by leaving whatever building it happens to be in when the command is given. The response has been generalised to cover a wide variety of situations which have something in common with each other. No one would suppose that the dog has constructed a generalised statement about the meaning of the command.

The suggestion is, then, that modes of moral thinking are subject to a process of generalisation in this sense. That is, they start out in young children as being highly specific, and similar situations are linked together so that, by the time maturity is reached, the mode of response is applied in a general way.

But, in talking about 'a response', we are simplifying the situation. There is not one mode of moral thinking, but four, and, as we have seen, older children have reasons for moral judgements which fall within more than one, or even all of them.

Let us consider a hypothetical case to see how this works out. Let us examine the development of an imaginary child's attitudes to bullying. It would be a mistake to suppose that the pre-school child has a unitary concept which corresponds to the adult idea of bullying. This is something that must wait until the appropriate stage in the development of his concepts. Instead, he acquires a series of specific prohibitions which are connected with the common idea of bullying only in the eyes of the adult. The pre-school child learns not about bullying, but about hitting the baby, pulling his sister's hair, fighting with the little boy next door, and so on.

It seems reasonable to suppose that the different modes of moral thinking are related to different patterns of discipline. We have, in fact, seen something of this sort in an earlier chapter when we discussed the difference in the timing of a punishment and the consequent appearance of either inhibitory responses or guilt. It is also reasonable to suppose that the various adults in a child's life will not be entirely consistent in the type of discipline used. We may thus find that our little boy acquires an irrational inhibition against hitting a baby, learns that he mustn't fight with the boy next door 'because I say so!', or with his cousin 'because I'll smack you if you do!', or learns not to pull his sister's hair because it upsets her. The small boy thus has four entirely different bases for thinking about specific situations connected with what we, as adults, recognise as the general concept of bullying. 'How confusing for him!', you may think, but this is not necessarily so. So long as he treats them as specific instances, there is no reason why their disparity should confuse him.

Now we have seen that responses tend to become generalised so that they apply to other situations resembling the one to which they originally related. The present example is a case which fits this perfectly: a response which relates to pulling sister's hair may well become generalised to apply to the whole idea of bullying. But so, of course, can any of the others. The final stage, then, is one in which the individual has a number of different and simultaneously existing modes of thought which relate to a given situation.

Such a picture of moral thinking may seem at first sight complicated and difficult to grasp, but this is largely because we are accustomed to regarding such alternative patterns of thought as being mutually exclusive. But the idea of simultaneously existing but different modes of thought not only fits in with the finding that older children give various different kinds of reason for the same moral judgement, but also echoes our everyday experience. Most of us refrain from stealing from a shop. Naturally, since the reader is a sensitive and intelligent person, this is because he has worked out that the consequences are harmful to the shopkeeper, and if his example were followed, to society in general. But it is *also* because he would go to prison if he were caught; *and also* because authority is against it; *and also* because he would be ashamed of himself if his friends knew; *and also* because he just feels it wouldn't be right. And so on.

It happens sometimes, of course, that different modes of moral thinking, when applied to the same problem, point to different courses of action. This is particularly the case in a modern mass society.

When we say that no single one of these modes of thought is developmentally prior to the others, it does not follow that they are *morally* equivalent. On the contrary, as we have seen, most moral philosophers would argue that the other-considering or altruistic mode is the best, and perhaps the only proper, basis for moral action. This type of moral thinking is, then, intimately concerned with the question of moral education. This brings us to one of the most important practical points arising from the use of different models of moral development. As we have already seen, if altruism is the last of a series of consecutive phases, it cannot be the subject of direct methods of moral education until the child is ready for that phase. If, on the other hand, the idea of parallel development is shown to be preferable, then a primitive form of altruism is already present, even in the youngest age groups, and the task of moral education is to some extent simplified, since we can approach the ultimate goal from the very beginning.

If the relationship between the four main modes of moral thought is not that of a consecutive series, is there some other form of relationship which can shed light on the question of moral development? A definitive answer to this question must wait for the full analysis of the material we have already described, but we may tentatively put forward the following idea as being consistent with what we know so far.

Progress towards generalisation of the modes of moral thinking can be summarised by describing three stages. There is nothing in the data to suggest the number three, which has been chosen simply because it is the smallest number of stages which will adequately illustrate the expected direction of development.

1. *Stage of specificity*

The child approaches each situation separately, using whichever mode of moral thought happened to figure in his learning about that situation. There is no generalisation, but equally no possibility of a conflict of values. The child sees nothing extraordinary in the fact that his reason for not bullying his sister is because it upsets her, while his reason for not bullying the baby is because 'it's just wrong'.

2. *Stage of overlap or partial generalisation*

When the process of generalisation has begun, not only does each mode of thinking relate to a wider group of situations which begin to resemble adult moral concepts, but also it has begun to overlap in its application with some of the other modes of thought. At this stage, then, the possibility of conflict of values appears for the first time.

3. *Stage of stability*

For those situations where conflict occurs, a 'peck-order' has been established between the various modes of thought, and a degree of stability has been attained. Most situations are still over-determined in the sense that there are a number of different modes of thinking which relate to them, but a preferred mode has probably emerged by this time, so that we can, in a limited way, at this stage use the modes of thought as a typology.

SUMMARY

The last two chapters have dealt with two basic approaches to the problem of children's moral development.

The first of these makes use of a simple model whereby the child passes through a small number of phases, the process being either consecutive or cumulative.

The second, which is a minority view, argues that the main types of moral thought are present from a very early age, and that each of them is subject to its own developmental sequence. It is further stated that the four types of response are subject to a generalisation effect, which results in moral judgements being over-determined or multi-causal.

Each of these approaches has important implications for moral education, but the second one implies that direct methods can be employed soon.

Ultimately, our choice between these two approaches must depend on the provision of further evidence.

FURTHER READING

See Williams (23).

7 Moral Development

In this book we have been able to look at only those few aspects of personality which have a direct and explicit bearing on moral behaviour; in a book of this length and scope, it is not possible to go beyond this in any detail. The existence of other aspects must however be constantly borne in mind, since the fact that their influence may be less direct does not reduce the importance of their contribution, either as components of moral behaviour or as prerequisites. Among these, we may pick out, in the former group, the development of social and interpersonal skills – such as empathy, communication, role playing – and personal skills – such as control of behaviour. As 'prerequisites' we may list intelligence, cognitive and conceptual skills, and such general attributes of personal development as mental health or maturity. All of these are topics which need to be followed up in detail by the student who intends to take the question of moral development and moral education beyond the stage of general interest. Some of these will be mentioned in passing in this chapter, but this will be scarcely more than an introductory sketch of each topic.

At the beginning of this book, it was suggested that moral development goes on in a number of directions at once, and that although we may need to consider these separately for reasons of convenience, it is not possible to form a true picture without examining the relationship between the various parts. We now need to attempt this task, and to try to give a global review, within a single chapter, of some of the characteristics of a child's moral development.

We have, of course, examined in an earlier chapter what were described as schemes of moral development. But these were, in fact, something different, being concerned rather more with a particular aspect of the topic, namely the child's style of thinking about moral problems, or his orientation towards morality. Questions of, for instance, those skills necessary for a particular attitude to result in consonant behaviour were necessarily excluded.

However, the interaction between the various aspects of development is not something which applies only within the sphere of moral development. It applies equally to the relationship between moral and general development. Moral development is only one aspect of the child's growth, and it may be profoundly affected by the course of other aspects of development – intellectual, emotional, social, and even, in some cases, physical. All of these are inextricably bound up with each other. Intellectual development, for instance, may be retarded by emotional disturbance, which may in turn be adversely affected by deficiencies in physical development. Or an individual may concentrate on intellectual accomplishment because his poor physique makes it impossible for him to compete in physical activities with any degree of success. Just as intellectual, social and emotional growth interact with each other, so any of them may affect the child's capacity for moral action, as we shall see in some of the specific instances discussed below.

INTELLECTUAL AND MORAL DEVELOPMENT

It may be that, in drawing attention to a connection between intellectual and moral development, we may appear to be saying that the most intelligent people are the most moral – or to put it in a more contentious form, only the clever can be good. Such a statement, of course, is offensive to many people, particularly to those who are attracted by the idea of the simple but good man, or the 'noble savage'. But of course such a notion is untrue, and nothing of the sort is implied by the original statement that the two are connected. After all, we can all think of people who are both clever and immoral.

It is true, on the other hand, that examination of the other end of the scale seems to point to a weak relationship of this kind:

if you examine delinquency rates, for example, you will find that the average level of intelligence of delinquents is significantly below that of the population as a whole. But there are a number of other factors which may contribute to this state of affairs. Intelligence tests tend to be influenced by social class, which is in turn reflected in the delinquency rate. Opportunity for success of a legitimate kind is more readily available to the more intelligent child. And it is also dangerous to make a simple equation between delinquency and lack of morality. Official figures necessarily relate to those forms of immoral behaviour which are also illegal (and also, of course, to those offenders who get caught, who may be less intelligent). On the whole, it seems that there is not a very good case for supposing that there exists a *simple* relationship between the two.

But this does not imply that they are entirely unrelated. Insofar as moral behaviour includes the idea of predicting the conse-quences of our actions and being responsible for them, anything which tends to diminish a person's power of making such pre-dictions tends also to diminish his responsibility and his capacity for moral action. The individual's intellectual capacity plays a great part in such prediction. The argument, then, is not that there is a direct relationship between intelligence and morality, but that there is a threshold below which such ideas as morality and responsibility are no longer applicable.

There is nothing new in this. The idea has long been embodied in the criminal law; those whose intellectual capacities fall below a certain level (admittedly not always easy to define) are deemed not to be responsible for their criminal actions. This applies not only to those whose responsibility is diminished by permanent defect, but to those who have not developed yet sufficiently to cross the threshold – children, in other words, below an arbitrarily defined age. (The new legislation on the age of responsibility seems, however, to be based on a somewhat different principle.)

Far from saying then that only the intelligent can be moral, the true state of affairs is that a person must attain a certain minimal level before his actions can be judged as either moral or immoral. And, of course, in this context, when we talk about intellectual capacity, we do not mean simply an individual's score on an intelligence test, but the whole array of cognitive and conceptu-alising ability which makes judgements involving consequences possible. For ordinary day-to-day experience, the kind of moral problem which faces all of us, this threshold is likely to be quite low. It is only when decisions on a grand scale are to be taken, whose consequences may affect many people and may stretch away far into the future, that the possession of the higher levels of intellectual capacity plays a more direct part in deciding whether the person can come to the right answer.

Now a great deal is known about the development of intelli-gence, and we can therefore apply this to moral development, since such information tells us what are the child's needs for an important prerequisite for moral behaviour. Intelligence is partly determined by heredity, but if we keep in mind the distinction between *genotypic* and *phenotypic* intelligence, we see that there is still plenty of room for important contributions by the child's early environment. Unfortunately, a few writers on education have tried recently to resurrect an old controversy about whether intelligence is acquired or inherited. The evidence which has been gathered together over the past thirty years points very clearly to the conclusion that it is not possible to discuss intellectual performance without reference to both of these factors.

In addition, then, to the child's innate intellectual potential, he needs an adequate environment if potential is to become reality. The environment should be stimulating (as we have already seen when discussing the effects of deprivation) and culturally and verbally rich. Recent work has shown that the level and type of verbal expression in the child's environment has profound and long lasting effects on both thinking style and thinking performance.

EMOTIONAL AND MORAL DEVELOPMENT

The relationship between emotional and moral development is of a similar nature to that which we have found in the case of intellectual development. The general picture is, however, more confused because there is a lack of clarity in the way the concept is used. This applies equally to the similar notions of maturity and mental health. Can one say that the more mature, or mentally healthy, or emotionally developed a person is, the more he is likely to be moral? Admittedly, it is possible to argue that an immoral person is necessarily emotionally immature or mentally unhealthy. This, of course, is the argument which lies behind much of our penal reform. It rests on the proposition that all adjusted people are moral, which does not exclude the possibility that some moral people are maladjusted. In fact, it is easy to imagine such a case; say, a man who is afflicted with violent and irrational rages, which he nevertheless rigorously controls on moral grounds – his poor adjustment can be measured in terms of the otherwise productive energy which is directed to this end.

But whether or not this general proposition can be maintained, it can be demonstrated that most forms of poor personal or emotional development do lead to some impairment of capacities relevant to moral behaviour. These may be of various kinds. As we have seen, in the case of the psychopath, they are concerned with the individual's orientation towards other people. In other cases, they may relate to his capacity to form an accurate and undistorted picture of events in the world around him, his capacity to control his impulses, and so on.

Thus, it is possible in this case, too, to claim that there is a threshold, a minimal level of emotional development, below which a person cannot fall without serious impairment of his ability to make responsible moral decisions and carry them out.

The young child's needs for a warm and consistent framework within which to form relationships and develop his emotional life are therefore relevant, too, to his moral development.

SOCIAL AND MORAL DEVELOPMENT

This is a wide topic, which merits a book of its own. Morality, in the sense that we have been discussing it in this book, is not something which is practised in isolation. Nor is it a question of a mechanical working out of the utilitarian equation of the greatest good for the greatest number. Morality is, among other things, an aspect of our relationship with other people. And anything which diminishes our ability to make such relationships successful diminishes also our capacity for moral action.

Of course, in the widest sense, all relationships may be regarded as part of social development, but the earlier, more personal relationships have already been mentioned in connection with the child's emotional development. In the narrower sense, we are concerned with the development of a number of abilities or skills which enable us to deal with other people. These include perceptual abilities, such as the ability to perceive what other people are feeling, what they like or dislike, and what is good for them. This may be either a direct interpretation of their behaviour, a reading of their facial expression and so on, or more generalised propositions about people in general.

There are also what we might call performance skills, which involve the ability to act towards other people in a way which is in accordance with our interpersonal morality. These include the ability to communicate with them, to act our roles appropriately, to cope with social rules.

As with so many aspects of growth, all of these things appear to rest on the very basic experiences we have already discussed. But they have their own, more specific needs, which appear at a stage. It must be obvious that the child cannot develop social skills in isolation. But, no matter how obvious this is, there is a surprising number of parents who, for various reasons, hold young children back from making social contacts with their peers. Consider this actual (and recent) case. An expensive modern house had been built in a village, and an expensive family had just moved in. 'It's such a pity,' the mother said, 'that there are no children here of —'s age for him to play with'. There were, in fact, about a dozen children of that age, but they were all farm labourers' children, or they lived in the council houses at the end of the village, so they didn't count, and the newly-arrived child lived a lonely little life in his own garden.

Young children need, then, adequate contact with their peers, and sufficient security and encouragement to enable them to experiment with social behaviour and social relationships. Without this, they will develop into the sort of person who means well, but who is no good with people. As we have said before, such a person can perhaps not be described as immoral, but his moral principles are so ineffective that they do no good to himself or anyone else.

NEEDS AND GOALS

Our next task is to attempt an overview which will summarise and show the interrelationships between the various elements which we have examined separately. Probably the most convenient way of approaching this is to think in terms of the child's developmental goals at various points in time, and of the corresponding needs which must be met if these goals are to be achieved. Fortunately, these can be listed in chronological order, since they each tend to relate most importantly to a particular developmental period. We should, however, be quite clear about what we are saying when listing needs and goals in this kind of sequence. If we say that a particular period is characterised by a need for security, that is not to say that security is unnecessary at other times. We are simply saying that, at this point, security assumes a peculiar importance for the child's moral development. It is as if, for instance, we were to describe the acquisition of reading skills as a major learning task of the younger primary school child. Obviously, learning to read continues after this period – particularly in the case of the more advanced skills, such as reading for reference. There is, though, a sense in which it is true to regard the task as crucial at the earlier stage: if a child fails then, all kinds of remedial measures will become necessary later.

What follows relates particularly to our present topic, but since the elements of child development follow similar patterns in all their aspects, much of it reflects, too, general theories of child development. Our overview of moral development may be regarded as falling under five headings.

1. *The infant*

Task: to establish the basis for concern.
Need: a warm, stable environment, within which to develop an emotional relationship.

The developmental tasks of this earliest phase of life are, as we have seen, a foundation upon which rest a whole series of later developments. We have argued that a concern for others is basic to the notion of interpersonal morality. The experience of an adequate and satisfying emotional relationship at this stage seems to be necessary for the later appearance of this sense of concern, no matter how much this may be transformed and widened in scope in later life. If the child's needs are not met at this stage, the effects on future moral development are indeed profound and widespread, affecting a large number of specific aspects of moral behaviour. Studies of psychopaths, whose personality deficiencies are usually regarded as stemming from environmental failure at this crucial stage, show that the resulting moral incapacity is virtually complete.

Although the theme will not be taken up again, it should always be remembered that the extension of this concern to increasing circles of people is a continuing process which accompanies all of the developmental tasks described below.

2. The toddler

Task: to relinquish the egocentric position.
Need: enough security and stability in the family environment to permit this step forward.

Concern, we have argued, is central to interpersonal morality. We have seen, too, that this general quality has been refined by Wilson into a specific component of moral behaviour, referred to as PHIL. This has been defined as not merely a concern for others, but also the sense (though not necessarily precisely formulated) that other people have interests and needs and feelings which are of equal validity to one's own.

The infant and the toddler are egocentric and omnipotent. They exist at the centre of their perceived universe, which has its being for their benefit. The task of reorientation involved in seeing oneself as merely one individual among others is a difficult one. The earlier stage of omnipotence, which is also paradoxically one of complete dependence, is a tempting and secure alternative to autonomy. The child will only make this step if he has the support of a secure environment, to which he knows he can return, and adults who are willing to relinquish the position whereby the child relies completely on them.

Here, too, we have a theme which makes its appearance at every stage, but which will not be reiterated. It is one aspect only of the commonplace that the problems of children are those of parents. We frequently find that, for a variety of reasons, parents are ambivalent about the child's progress to autonomy, tending to hold him back for reasons which relate not to the child's needs but to their own personality. It is a problem that appears again when the child begins school, and in a more dramatic form when adolescence is reached and the person who was once the dependent baby begins to try out adult behaviour patterns. We can do no more here than draw attention to this widespread tendency, and affirm the complexity of the motivation that may lie behind it. It represents yet another strand which accompanies the later tasks described in this chapter.

3. The pre-school child

Task: establishing the elements of control.
Need: suitable models in the adult world.

The psychological nature of the mechanism by which control is effected remains obscure. Probably there are a number of such mechanisms involved in different cases. Anna Freud's work on the mechanisms of defence points to some aspects of control at an unconscious level. Of relevance, too, is the work on imitation referred to in an earlier chapter.

Task: the establishment of the modes of moral thought.
Need: adults who communicate.

The traditional view of this period of moral development is one which would see the main task as being the establishment of conscience in either of its senses. It is undoubtedly true that this is a major event of this period, but other styles, or habits of thought, appear to date from this time, too. These, as we have seen, are concerned with heteronomous, expedient and altruistic approaches to morality. They undergo changes which reflect the child's increasing power of thought and conceptualisation.

4. *The school child*

Task: to reconcile and generalise the modes of moral thought.

It would be premature to make a firm statement about the needs for this task, since this is the subject of ongoing research.

Task: to learn social skills.
Need: an adequately stimulating social environment, which will enable him to try out various roles and skills. Of course, much of this activity has its origins in behaviour which was learnt towards the end of the previous phase, but this is the great learning period.

We have already said enough about the relevance of social skills to make it unnecessary to enlarge on this point.

5. *The adolescent*

Tasks: (*a*) to establish a flexible interrelationship between the modes of moral thought.

    (*b*) to weld these into moral principles which relate to the real world of adults.

    (*c*) to reappraise earlier methods of moral problem solving where necessary.

    (*d*) to adapt them so that they are applicable to adult problems which are new to the adolescent. These are not only to do with the newly-awakened sexual instincts, but also to do with the emergence of adult skills, and, a little later, the entry into the world of work.

Any account of the problems of the adolescent in this field must be read against the general background of the period, which involves a drastic reorganisation of the personality at a physical, emotional and social level.

Moral development and moral education are important subjects. If the studies summarised here show us anything, it is that the child's progress at every stage, and in every direction, can have a bearing on his capacity for moral action in adult life. Those who have the care of children and adolescents, of whatever age, cannot evade responsibility for the child's progress in this sphere.

H

Conventionally, a book of this sort finishes with some kind of resounding and memorable conclusion. This will not be attempted here. The subject is of such importance and, unfortunately, of such difficulty that it is better to think in terms not of a conclusion but of an introduction.

SUMMARY

The various aspects of moral development cannot be viewed in isolation from each other, nor can moral development as a whole be separated from the context of the child's general development. Intellectual, social and emotional development are all relevant to some degree.

FURTHER READING

See Stone (24), Mussen (25), and Williams (26).

Bibliography

Dimensions of moral behaviour
General accounts of the dimensional approach to personality may be found in

1. Cattell, R. B. *The Scientific Analysis of Personality* (Penguin 1965)
2. Eysenck, H. J. *Fact and Fiction in Psychology* (Penguin 1965)

For a discussion of generality and specificity in moral behaviour, the principal source is, of course,

3. Hartshorne, H. & May, M. A. *Studies in the Nature of Character* (Macmillan (USA) 1929)

This, however, is difficult to obtain. Brief discussions of the topic may be found in

4. Eysenck, H. J. *Crime and Personality* (Routledge 1964)
5. Wilson, J., Williams, N. & Sugarman, B. N. *Introduction to Moral Education* (Penguin 1967)

The latter also includes a full discussion of the components of moral behaviour.

Concern
A general account of the effects of maternal deprivation is

6. Bowlby, J. *Child Care and the Growth of Love* (Penguin 1953)

To correct the balance, however, this should be read in conjunction with the later collection of papers.

7. Ainsworth, Mary D. *et al. Deprivation of Maternal Care: A Reassessment of its Effects* (WHO 1962)

For a discussion of egocentricity and growth of autonomy, see

8. Erikson, Erik H. *Childhood and Society* (Penguin 1965)

Conscience

A very clear account of the problems in this area is given in the relevant chapter of

9. Brown, Roger *Social Psychology* (Free Press 1967)

Other important sources are

10. Stephenson, G. M. *The Development of Conscience* (Routledge 1966)
11. Aronfreed, J. *Conduct and Conscience* (Academic Press 1968)
12. Flugel, J. C. *Man, Morals and Society* (Penguin 1955)
    Eysenck, H. J. *op. cit.*
13. Freud, S. *Two Short Accounts of Psychoanalysis* (Penguin 1966)
14. Freud, A. *The Ego and the Mechanisms of Defence* (Hogarth Press 1954)
15. Sears, R. R., Maccoby, E. E. & Levin, H. *Patterns of Child Rearing*, Evanston, Ill. (Row Peterson & Co. 1957)
16. Riesman, D. *et al. The Lonely Crowd* (Yale University Press 1950)

The reader should certainly look at

17. Piaget, J. *The Moral Judgment of the Child* (Routledge 1932)

Those who have little acquaintance with Piaget's work might however be well advised to look first at some introductory text, such as

18. Brearley, M. & Hitchfield, E. *A Teacher's Guide to Reading Piaget* (Routledge 1966)
19. Piaget, N. Isaacs *Some Answers to Teachers' Questions* (National Froebel Foundation 1965)
20. Peck, R. F. & Havighurst, R. J. *et al. The Psychology of Character Development* (Wiley (USA) 1960)
21. Kohlberg, L. 'The Development of Children's Orientations Towards a Moral Order. I: Sequence in the Development of Moral Thought', *Vita Humana*, 6 (1963)
22. Kay, W. *Moral Development* (Allen & Unwin 1968)

Modes of moral thought

23. Williams, N. 'Children's Moral Thought. Part I: Categories of Moral Thought', *Moral Education*, 1 (1) (1969)
    'Part II: Towards a Theory of Moral Development', *Moral Education*, 1 (2) (1969)

Development
A general book on child development would be a useful start.

24. Stone, L. J. & Church, J. *Childhood and Adolescence* (Random House (USA) 1957)
25. Mussen, P. L. *The Psychological Development of the Child* (Prentice Hall (USA) 1963)
26. Williams, N. *Child Development* (Heinemann 1969)

Moral Philosophy
Discussions of some of the topics of this book from the philosophical viewpoint will be found in:

27. Atkinson, R. F. *Conduct: An Introduction to Moral Philosophy* (Macmillan 1969)

Note that the above references are not always to the original edition. Bearing in mind the readership of this book, preference has been given, where there is a choice, to paperbacks and other easily obtained editions.

Index